Hello, GRACE

Forgiveness for a Sinful Saint

TOVIYAH J.

WESTBOW
PRESS®
A DIVISION OF THOMAS NELSON
& ZONDERVAN

WestBow Press books may be ordered through booksellers or by contacting:

WestBow Press
A Division of Thomas Nelson & Zondervan
1663 Liberty Drive
Bloomington, IN 47403
www.westbowpress.com
1 (866) 928-1240

ISBN: 978-1-9736-0522-5 (sc)
ISBN: 978-1-9736-0523-2 (hc)
ISBN: 978-1-9736-0521-8 (e)

Library of Congress Control Number: 2017914996

Print information available on the last page.

WestBow Press rev. date: 08/30/2019

Foreword

"Even though I walk through the darkest valley, I will fear no evil, for you are with me; your rod and your staff, they comfort me."

Psalm 23:4 *NIV*

Contents

PART ONE

In the Beginning

CHAPTER 1

Home

"E DIDE, SKOOL TI YA." It's 5:30am. My mother's slight tap and warm voice wakes me up along with my two older siblings. Her phrase says to get up because it's time for school. Whether we were at church or at my grandmother's house, we had to bathe outside. The bathrooms at either place did not accommodate a bathing tub. My mother would heat up water on the stove to mix with the cold tap water in a bucket. She would rapidly scrub our bodies with the hard sponge and pour the warm water from our heads down.

The bus stop loomed.

We made haste to get there before the entry lines got long and unbearable. Although she learned to drive, a motor accident discouraged Ma from driving again. Despite mild injuries to the person she hit with the car in the accident, Ma was traumatized enough to stop driving.

For some time, we were fortunate to have a driver that chauffeured us to and from school. When funds waned from my father abroad, we could no longer afford the driver and the car. Consequently, we used public transportation. Ma often rode with us on the bus and dropped us off at school before she headed to her secretarial job. Aside from that job, she also owned a quaint shop in one of the local market centers. She still manages that shop today. I didn't know then that my mother was doing the work of two. She was a single parent because of my father's absence. Raising us, nurturing us, and taking care of our daily routines were her part and I was too young then to fully understand the toll it took on her.

Fortunately, my siblings and I went to the same school. Ma tried to have us consistent in our punctuality. When the bus reached our stop by the school corner, we often ran to get in line for the student call every morning, as it was the routine of the private institution we attended. Lateness warranted lashes on the backs of students who were not in line when the morning procession began.

My father owned the land that housed our home, but we rarely resided there after he traveled. My mother insisted that it was for security and distance reasons. So, we often stayed with my Grandma Alhaja (Al-haa-ja) or slept at church. Either way, our young backs got accustomed to hard floors. Fortunately, thin sleeping mats separated our bodies from the floors.

When we stayed at church for extensive periods, Ma did her best to protect us from the ants and night-flies. In the designated area we slept, she placed a chair at each corner of the large, rectangular mat we slept on. She would create a tent-like covering with a large net, looping each of the four corners of the net, through each chair. It was her best attempt to keep the mosquitoes from feasting on our bodies while we slept.

At least once a month, Ma took us to her job. We used her office phone to call my father. Since we didn't own a home phone, this was our primary mode of communication with him. We all looked forward to those trips. After about an hour and a half, we would take the long trip back to wherever we were sleeping that week. Often, it was at church because the distance to school was much shorter from there.

We were in church a lot. We practically lived there. Ma was always working and running around to get money grams from my father. She did her best to make us feel safe and secure. She really was superwoman. She never complained and I never once heard a bitter utterance come out of my mother's mouth over having to raise us while our father was in America. She was a devoted mother who made sure we never lacked love, care, or anything else we needed.

I was not so young to miss the hectic life that Ma juggled. I saw that she carried everyone's burden, especially her family's own. Since she was the first born of six, traditionally, the responsibility rested on her shoulders to look after everyone else, including her parents. That, she did well. I learned in my older years that Ma couldn't pursue higher education because of this obligation as first born. She was the one who began working soon after she finished high school and later financed her youngest sibling's schooling. She was the one who made a necessary sacrifice seeing as my uncle, the youngest of her siblings, was the only male child in the family and it felt necessary for him to obtain higher education as the man in the family.

Ma's burden seemingly never lifted. Even after they were all grown up, it seems my mother still bore the weight of responsibility of her family. She paid my grandfather's medical bills and gave my grandmother groceries funds to feed and cater to everyone in the household. Some of my cousins that stayed with my grandmother also ate from what my mother provided. At other times, Ma extended financial help to this sister, then the other. I never saw her stop. I rarely ever saw her sleep. I marvel at the strength of God that carried my mother as she carried everyone else around her.

When her father passed away, Ma's strength and poise kept things going as preparations were made for his funeral. His passing shattered my little heart because his was the first death I experienced so closely. I was six years old. While most of us wallowed with our broken hearts, my mother stood strong and took care of every detail that needed attention. She was the one who shared laughter and prayers reminding us that grandpa was of old age and he lived a full life. Ma also helped us understand that death was natural in old age and we should celebrate the life grandpa lived rather than cry endlessly about his passing. I didn't know then how to express the ache my heart felt knowing that I would never dance with my grandfather again. Since I didn't get the chance to meet my father's father, "baba," had been the only grandpa I had. *Baba* was the first dead person I had ever seen. My mother said a prayer over his body as we gathered around him on burial day. As strange as it was, I did not feel fear standing beside his lifeless body completely wrapped up in white. I even remember the smell of the blue cologne they dressed him in. God rest his sweet soul.

Grandpa wasn't the only man I missed dearly. I missed my own father's presence as a little girl. Many days came when sudden sadness would fill my space. On those days, I was often mute and very sad. I felt his absence. In the five years he was abroad, it seemed death was all around me. Too many people passed away. I don't recall which happened when, but it felt like years of mourning. Grandpa passed, then my youngest uncle on my father's side passed. Then it was my father's oldest brother. Then my father's sister. Then the closest person I had to a godmother. No other death broke my heart more than the sudden death of my dear uncle Deola (Day-Oh-La). His was the most unexpected tragedy of all. The entire church community was not prepared to bury a newly wedded man whose wife had given birth to triplets less than two years earlier. His passing indeed broke many hearts. The pain was so unbearable that this time my mother wept profusely.

CHAPTER 2

Innocence

I FELL SICK IN THE immediate months following my father's departure to America. My mother, in the custom of Yoruba belief, clothed me with his shirts hoping I'd get well sooner than later. My sickness got worse before it got better. I burned with high fever for many nights and refused to eat. When I did eat, I vomited it all during the midnight hours. I was ill for about a month. And although healing came to my body, my young heart still felt the void of a missing parent especially when my innocence was threatened.

The first time was at the house we rarely stayed in, the one my father completed before his trip abroad. We got along well with our next-door neighbors and my brother and I often played with them till my mother returned home from work. On this day, everyone was outside in my neighbor's small goods shop that was perched right by the front of their house. I went inside my neighbor's house to lay down and read. When I heard the door open, I shifted my gaze away from the book in my hand to see a familiar face.

He was my neighbor's relative.

When he closed the door behind him and moved closer to where I was, I wasn't bothered at first. That was until I heard a zipper. I was laying faced down with my head hovered over the book when I felt rough hands grip my shoulders. He turned me over and attempted to pin me down, but his grip wasn't strong enough to pin my whole body down on the mattress. I don't recall what he was saying, but I remember disagreeing with every word and fighting my way from under him. I don't remember screaming, just fighting. I wouldn't be still. I heard the terrified sound of my rapid heartbeat. I was in danger but something in me told me to fight back. So, I did. I moved my body left and right, pushed at his chest, moved my face from side to side, moved my knees without control, and did everything I could think of to prevent stillness of my body. I could tell from his frown and confused look that he had not expected me to fight him as hard. I had not expected to fight as hard. I soon felt his resolve weaken after a few moments of our tussle. When I felt his body ease away briefly from mine, I shoved harder at his chest one last time with all the energy I had in my seven-year-old body and ran outside. I told no one.

It happened again with another man.

I was staying with my grandma, Alhaja. The family-owned hospital across her housing complex often opened the doors to its playhouse and invited many of the neighborhood children to watch TV and play for a little while. That night, when it was time to leave, we all dispersed and went to our various abodes. Once at home, I realized that I left my new digital watch at the hospital residence. It was a green and black 7up watch that I won from a promotion the week before. I loved the watch and wore it everywhere, so I didn't want to leave it overnight even if it was across the street.

After my fussing and feigned tears, Ma agreed for my nanny to walk over with me to retrieve my watch. I'm unsure why she refused to come all the way to the back with me because she stayed by the gate while I went into the playhouse.

The hospital security guard, Rah, walked with me from the gate to the backhouse where we had all been a few hours earlier. I found the watch, picked it up, and eagerly walked toward the gate. I walked a few feet away from the playhouse ahead of Ray. He stopped me and asked for a hug. I obliged momentarily before he abruptly picked me up. Rah was tall and lean, but his grip was harsh and frightening. He asked for a kiss. I shook my head. He then kissed my cheek and asked if I would lay down on the ground. I said no. He insisted. I said no. But he wouldn't put me down. He tried to lay me down on the ground while still hugging me. At that time, my nanny started calling my name. Rah insisted that it'd be quick if I just lay down. I said no and began my fight. Just like the first time, I writhed and shook my shoulders and pushed away at another intruder's chest. I was scared but I wouldn't stay still, and I wouldn't lay on the ground.

After about two minutes of scuffling against his perverted gestures, I got worried. Rah was relentless in having his way with me on the cold brick hospital ground. My worry shifted when I heard the hospital watch-dog barking, which alarmed and distracted Rah. My nanny's voice, now louder than it was a few moments prior, stirred up the dog at that hour of the night. A barking dog would alarm the entire hospital to thinking something was wrong, so I knew my attacker had to go quiet the dog. Thank God for a barking dog. I could tell Rah was still thinking about what to do because he was still holding on to me close to the ground rather than getting up to attend to the dog. Without thinking too much about what was possible, I broke free from his grip and ran to the gate like my life depended on it. I never went back to the playhouse.

Once again, I never told anyone.

Young girls are stripped of their sense of safety, virtue and innocence forcefully and often unexpectedly. It was a frightening reality and it dawned on me how unsafe the world was. It happened so often all around me in Nigeria. This was childhood.

After some months, it happened again.

The clubhouse was where all the young kids hung out. Sometimes, no one was there. This afternoon, I wanted some sweets, but I didn't have the money to get some. My brother, sister, and cousins were nowhere to be found. Since I was the youngest of the bunch, I was often left behind to stay home with Alhaja anyway. I went to the clubhouse to see if any of the other kids were around. None of them were there but one of the men that lived in the complex was present. I asked if he had any change to spare so I could get some sweets. He said he did.

I should have said no. I knew enough at seven-years-old to not go into any room with any man. This time, I did as I was instructed and followed him to get the money. There was an unsettling feeling in my stomach when I stepped in the room and watched him close the door behind him. I immediately asked for the change without offering small conversation. I wanted to stay by the door, but he took my hand and led me to the bed. He sat down on the bed. While still holding my hand, saying something and nothing at the same time, he told me to lift my dress while he pulled out his member and lowered my panties. Not again I thought. Would it really happen this time around? Would I be able to get away? What if I tried to fight and he hurt me even worse? Will there be a lot of blood?

I was standing with my dress raised up and both my hands shaking quietly accepting what seemed like the inevitable. I thought to myself how this happened all the time to girls my age around here. Perhaps it was bound to happen to me too sooner or later. I stared intently at the window above his bed, silently praying that someone would walk by or a knock would come. I hoped for someone to call my name again. I needed something to happen to make this not happen.

The moment he proceeded to get closer to me, we heard footsteps. My assaulter's startled response was enough to let me know that I had been saved for the third time. I walked as fast as my young legs would carry me toward the door and headed outside. I didn't see who it was that stepped into the clubhouse and I didn't stop to inquire. I kept walking hoping to get as far away as physically possible. In the calm of having escaped yet again, a blur came over my innocence. It was hard to say how far I could go without losing it eventually.

The following year, something different happened. I had an idea of what it meant for two people to touch one another. At eight years old, I was overwhelmed and encouraged by my curiosity to know what it felt like. I didn't know what it was but the closest description I can give to it, is that it felt like a strong invisible itch. I felt my body wanting to feel things and do things I didn't feel like doing before. Growing up in a culture that set a taboo on speaking of sexuality or anything close to it before the age deemed 'appropriate,' I regretted thinking or feeling as I did and although I was ashamed of it, I still couldn't shake it off. No one told me that puberty was here. No one told me that the changes in my thought process was really my body relating the message that it was about to undergo a transition into early womanhood.

I didn't miss the illicit language that referenced sex in all my environments. I was alert enough to know when the older kids gathered around in a circle to talk and joke about it. I closely observed young couples when they kissed with affection and often wondered how far they went with each other. This was my 'sex education.' So, as I embraced the urge to do, that thought of what it meant to touch and be touched by a boy gradually encouraged me to act on that forbidden urge.

That day at school, the audacity abruptly sprung up. I knew there was a thin line between my curiosity and my rebellion, but the lines overlapped when I asked a classmate during lunch hour, if he wanted to come to the bathroom with me. He said yes.

We didn't get far.

It didn't matter what was done or almost done, someone caught us and that meant trouble. I went to a private school. Aside from the painful disciplinary lashes that would fall on my back, there were other consequences to worry about. What would my mother do or say? Would I be expelled? Suspended? Would I be made an example of in front of the whole school? The thoughts of all kind of punishment filled my head as I pleaded earnestly with the older boy that caught us. I begged profusely and explained that nothing was done no matter what was intended. But there was no appealing to this boy. I knew that day that he would use this against me, but I had no idea that it would be in worse ways than lashes or expulsion.

This older student was cruel. I became indebted to him in return for his secrecy. That same day, he demanded that I met with him after school hours in the bathroom so I could show him what I and my accomplice from earlier had originally planned to do before he came knocking. He threatened to tell the headmaster if I refused to meet him. So, I went. I knew he was up to no good, but I was convinced that this was the repercussion I had to face for my perverted interest in the first place.

That day, he touched me.

It was not forcefully violent, but it was un-welcomed, and he knew it. I stood silently as he touched me. I felt violated and dirty. I hoped it'd be the only time and that I wouldn't have to expose myself to him again after that. It wasn't.

The threats and the blackmail came the following week as this older boy demanded all my lunch money and snacks. Days, weeks, and months went by with my lunch becoming his lunch. When he missed a day at school, he expected me to hold my lunch money and give it to him when I saw him. I was often hungry after school and during the long trips home but would not dare tell my sister or brother. On some desperate days, I lied and said I misplaced my money or I had to borrow someone. As uncomfortable as it was to give my lunch allowance up every day, I didn't complain so long as I didn't have to meet the older kid in the bathroom again.

The second time around, when he demanded that I met him after school, it was him and a friend in the bathroom. I remained in silence as they both touched me.

I kept my silence and endured the torture that school now represented for me. Some days I wished I was stronger and bolder. I wished I could tell someone why I now hated school but there was none to tell, at least not without the risk of everything coming out in the open. There were days I wished bad things on the older boy and days I hoped he wouldn't come to school again. But this boy was always there, always threatening, always taking.

Once or twice, I felt the courage to defy his requests and I dared him to tell on me. As soon as I did that, he listed the many consequences that I'd face should the headmaster or any other authority find out about my past intent with my classmate. I was never brave enough to let him go through with it. Besides, I felt responsible for asking my accomplice to come with me and I knew that we would both be punished if word was to ever get out. I didn't want that. Daily, I caved to the demands of my blackmailer.

That was the most painful schoolyear of my childhood, if I could still call it that. With all that my young eyes had seen by then, childhood seemed to have eluded me. It was not until a few years into my teenage years that I acknowledged that I had been molested, bullied, and blackmailed in that time. Still, no one saw it and no one stopped it.

Where was my brother, sister, or mother during that time? Why did I feel so alone? Why was there no one to tell so they could defend me? These questions followed me as the years passed and I learned then to face my troubles without relying on anyone to rescue me.

My blackmailer eventually switched schools the following year, but a sense of dread kept me company and almost made me forget he was gone. I was terrified that he would one-day pop up in class and the blackmail or molest would begin again. But he never did, and I never told anyone.

CHAPTER 3

A One-Way Flight

AMERICA WAS THE CLOSEST THING to heaven on earth for any Nigerian-born person like me. Many of us were told as children what a spectacular place it was, like a world on its own. Growing up, many of us believed that America was certainly the land of everything possible, including special people with blue and green eyes. America was like magic, a paradise in this world as portrayed by anyone who talked about it.

For many Nigerians, going to America was a great feat and accomplishment. The most affluent people in the country sent their children abroad for the best education and those we read about were connected to America in one way or another.

So, when my father left Nigeria for this enchanted place, I felt very special. A flood of visitors visited our home in the two weeks before my father's departure. I remember the adult huddles during those visits where three or four respectable elders in my church community gathered together with their adult drinks and talked for hours. My young awareness revealed that something major was going on and that something big was about to happen. I was four years old when he traveled. My mother encouraged me to be proud to know that although my father wouldn't be around to carry me around and watch me blossom, he would be somewhere most people in our country only dreamed of going.

There was a void at home. The fragrance of my dad's cologne stung the air and I felt his absence in the aroma of the faint vapor. My father was no longer with me and I was aware of it. Much like his scent, the excitement about America soon faded and my sickness followed. I remember being prayed over, having visitors, and visiting a minister's home for a long period. Since it was in the Yoruba custom to avoid hospitals unless necessary, I was not carried to the hospital. Rather, I was carried to the church leader's home to be prayed over and nurtured back to good health. Although my father visited two or three times in the five years we lived in separate countries, it did little to assuage the ache of missing him in my life. I was glad when the five years of separation came to an end.

CHAPTER 4

Far Away

THE COLD DECEMBER AIR GREETED me in New York after our plane landed at JFK in December 2001. I was elated at the feel of the coldest chill I ever felt on my skin.

That chilly day in December, I ran as fast as I could into my father's open arms and greeted him as though I had not seen him at all in the five years we were apart. It was a special moment. It felt surreal to finally set my feet in America to be with my father again. I missed him very much. I missed his gentle and calm nature in the years he was absent in Nigeria. I even missed his serene admonishment of our bad behavior when my siblings and I gave my mother trouble.

My joy to be in America and my love for my father didn't prepare me for the new world into which I was thrust. I started school less than a month after I came in the country with my two older siblings, Mike and Mayus. Luckily for Mike, he already had an English name and would not face the challenge of finding a suitable 'American' name. Since Mayus and I didn't have English names, my father initiated picking one suitable for an American classroom. He inferred that our names were too difficult to pronounce here and could hinder our smooth navigation into the culture. I picked the name, 'Angelina', Mayus picked the name, 'Roslyn'.

Back then, it only appeared as a mere name change, but an

identity battle quickly ensued without my own awareness. It felt great renaming me. I felt American. Mayus was thirteen, Mike was twelve, and I was nine. All three of us began school the second week of January. That's essentially when the separation began, one that molded the dynamics of our new family structure now that we were with our father but without our mother. I was placed in the fourth grade, Mike in the seventh, and Mayus in the eighth. An oldest sibling who was slightly older than Mayus, was also in America with us.

I always knew I had an older sibling from my father's previous marriage before my mother, but I had only met my half-sister once or twice prior to our meeting again in America. I initially felt strange to now reside in the same house with her. Still, I was eager to finally become familiar with an older sister that was always kept at a distance from the family back when we were in Nigeria. On the surface, I didn't have much to relate to with Liz, who is about seven years my senior, but we were very similar in likes and mannerisms. Living with Liz was short-lived because she ventured out of the home on her own two years later. That separation came to have lasting effects on the bonds of our relationship. As much as I needed all the sisters I could get, I was compelled to settle for my sense of lack in the beginning of my teenage years.

I am probably the only girl I know who marveled at the idea of a basement home. 'An underground house,' was how my father described it. As an adolescent, I was in awe that such accommodations even existed. There were stairs that went under the house structure from the outside and was technically below ground level. We lived in the one-bedroom, one-bathroom basement for about three and a half years. There was a living room and a kitchen area so we had all we needed. The girls shared the one room while Mike had a bed in the space provided in the boiler room. I found out a few months into living in our basement, that the entire house was under my father's name. While we lived in the basement quarters, my father had a tenant whose family occupied the living areas upstairs.

The first few weekends after our arrival to America, Dad made it a mission to have Fridays as our family quality time together. Since he worked three different jobs, he was rarely home. And when he was home, he had to catch up on rest to prepare for his overnight security job. When he did sleep for a couple of hours during the day, we all, especially Mike, felt the cramp of habituating in such a confined space. My brother would often have to sleep on the living room couch while my father would sleep in the boiler room, where a twin-sized spring mattress was set up. Life was not peachy, but we did not fail to count our blessings. So, I looked forward to Fridays. My father would come home from work, pick Mike, Mayus, and I up, then we would all go pick Liz from her job at Blockbuster. Liz used her discount to rent out movies we could all watch for the night. Then we would all go to Dunkin Donuts or some other eatery to grab snacks and dinner to eat while we enjoyed the movies. These were the closest times we ever did get to spend together as a family.

Weeks went by and America started to feel more permanent. I was growing up in America. It was really happening, and I no longer had to make up stories for my classmates about my fantasies of coming to America someday. I was usually happy at heart until the need for my mother came about. I tried hard to get along with my new life and new normal without my mother's presence in the home, but it didn't take long to feel the great void. Ma didn't explain to me how painful cramps would be when my menstrual cycle came. Ma didn't teach or watch me cook my first soup and meal at the age of ten. Ma didn't purchase my very first bra, sanitary napkins, nor the necessary pain medication I needed. Ma didn't teach me to wash my clothes at the laundromat nor take me shopping every school year. Ma wasn't around to tuck me in at night, pick out my attire for school, comb my hair, or make me breakfast. Ma was in Nigeria and I had to live with that.

It was my father who did most of these things as his schedule permitted. I know he tried to be present but there were obligations that demanded he carried the weight of three jobs while feeding five mouths, including his own. I was old enough to see the sacrifices a hard-working man made, so we too learned to sacrifice to make the family work. America was a life without Ma as Nigeria was a life without my father.

There were no pictures taken on my first day of school. I felt unprepared, scared, confused, and anxious. I had not practiced my American accent long enough. My hair wasn't tidy enough, and I didn't know what to expect. Fortunately, I was a Nigerian girl whose first language was English. Still, my nerves were unsettled. I knew that my comfort in America would soon be tested, shifted, and challenged in many ways.

At school, my thick accent and foreign attitudes quickly stood out. At first, I didn't feel beautiful in the American sense but remained confident enough in how I looked. That quickly dissipated in the cruel and arrogant atmosphere of American kids who had no sense of relation or familiarity with an African girl or the culture she came from. My sense of self didn't keep the bullying from coming my way. My hair was short, so it was harder to keep my coarse strands flat and neat. Ma was in Nigeria and Mayus was doing her best to keep up with her new life in America too. I didn't know how to present my beauty. I did what I could to be presentable, but it seemed I never measured up. The cruel lips of many peers claimed that I was the ugly, bald African with lips that were too big for her face. I was the poor foreigner who could not afford the cool trending clothes. I was the outsider from the country that was portrayed on TV as dirty and impoverished.

Navigating 4th grade was indeed tough and painful.

The short years finishing up elementary school were filled with uncountable confrontations with kids at school who always had something new to tease me about. Every day was differently met with one bullying encounter after another. That was the sum of my first two years as the star of my American dream.

Nonetheless, amid the growing agony of my youth, I fell in love with two department stores at the age of twelve – The Dollar store and the thrift store. Both stores had a lot to offer a girl who grew up with many hand-me-downs. So, every new school year when my father delegated our individual budget to buy something new for school, I would first ask to be driven to my two favorite stores to see my options. It didn't matter that they were not name brands or as trendy as expected by my peers. All I cared about was the option to buy something that was new for me. Sixty dollars was not much, but it was what my father could afford, and I was grateful that something, anything new would touch my skinny frame the new school year.

During my fifth-grade year, I participated in the annual Martin Luther King speech contest. The auditioning process was gruesome. Admittedly, I felt like I was the least tidy-looking out of all the contestants. No one in my family was present in the audience but I advanced to the final round and won second place. Few days later in the school hallways, I overheard the conversation of two of my peers. One of the girls in the conversation confessed to the other how she heard one of the speech coordinators refer to me as the 'ugly African girl," during the competition. That was painful to hear. I'm unsure if she was being truthful or not. I didn't react too bad to it because I had gotten used to be the 'ugly African girl' indeed. I saw how many of the other girls in my peer set looked and I couldn't compare. I wished I knew any nearby salons or anyone who could neat my hair up. I was not familiar with any place. It probably wouldn't have mattered much anyway since I had no money to pay for a professional treatment of my hair. It just wasn't a priority for my hard-working father who estimated that having two older female siblings would afford me a descent hairstyle because they would help me do my hair, which rarely happened.

As much as my father advocated my adapting to American life, his strict and rigid Yoruba parenting reminded me of all things un-American at home. There was a tug between the identity that I was supposed to be away from home amongst American kids and the one that I was expected and mandated to be in my Nigerian household. I was diligent and clean in hygiene but the insults from school bullies often made me feel as though I was unclean. It sometimes felt like my existence polluted their presence and it angered them. Many of them never made me forget that no matter how polished I appeared with help from dollar-store hair creams and the thrift store's finest clothing, I would never be applauded for trying and I could never be counted as one of them.

Some kids got mad about having to sit next to me during lunch or on the bus during a school trip. In class, some of them muffled laughter and snickers when I raised my hand to answer a question. Sometimes, someone would correct my English accent when I said a word wrong or if my thick accent carried over in my statement. Some kids would simply talk about me in the lunch room when I was only a table away. Soon enough, the embarrassment and pressure of being the African piece in an American puzzle became so heavy that a raw cry for help came out of me the following year.

PART TWO
LOOSED BONDS

CHAPTER 5

Silent Tears

No one thought much of my sleep pattern during my fifth grade year. I told my father that I wasn't sleepy at night. Consequently, it was harder to stay awake during the day. My father soon received notes from my teacher that I fell asleep often in class, but it was not cause for much alarm since my grades were good. Time passed and my sleeplessness at night got worse. I learned the following school year that I was suffering from a chronic disorder called insomnia. Since it was not a life-threatening disease or something that could really be cured away, there was really no way to handle the matter. My father tried to mandate a TV cut-off time on school nights but it didn't help because I still laid sleepless on my bed way past midnight on most nights.

When sleep eluded me, I often thought about Ma and how much I missed her nurturing, affection, and loving presence. I thought about my church friends back in Nigeria and how I didn't have to worry about my speech back home since we all spoke the same way. I reminisced about the games we all played and how simpler life had been back home in Nigeria. Here in America, life was diluted. There was the liberty to experience more as a child but the restriction of my home life regulated that freedom. My inner child was lost. I couldn't find her. Every day at school was serious for me because I had to wear my defense each day. I was ready for a confrontation at any moment. I was always on edge with my tongue readily equipped with a response to the next bully.

When fifth grade ended, I felt drained of life's happiness. I was exhausted of fighting with words every day against kids. I was not looking forward to another schooling experience under the same conditions. I didn't attend my fifth-grade graduation. Admittedly, my father didn't consider it a big deal so I tried not to as well. Besides, the costs of buying a graduation dress, shoes, and getting my hair done felt like too much to ask of my father. So, I played down my disappointment and focused on the near future. I had not yet shared with my father the voices that were starting to talk about killing myself in my head.

After the summer break, I started middle school. School was a few weeks in and I was excited about starting sixth grade because it made me feel older.

This day, it had been another lost battle with a request from my father. My father broke yet another promise to me. He said he would do something and did not. Feeling defeated, I cried hysterically. I was angry and hurt. None of my siblings comforted me. No one hugged me and said they understood my frustration. No one pat me on the back to say it would be okay. I was hurt and I felt ignored.

In tears, I went in the room with my sister's deactivated phone and dialed 9-1-1.

Something about hearing the voice of someone on the other line who was concerned about my tears brought me relief. Not sure exactly what I felt relieved from but it was there and I embraced it. I just wanted somebody to hear me and not shut me up. I wanted somebody to listen. I wanted somebody to tell me that my voice mattered. I wanted comfort. I needed comfort.

The thin wall that separated the rooms was not sound-proof nor was the bedroom fully closed. Yet no one stopped me. No one interrupted my brief conversation with the operator. No one in the house heard me give the stranger over the phone our home address after my confession that I needed someone to talk to and I was contemplating suicide. A unit was sent over to the house.

Shortly before the cops arrived, I confessed to my father and siblings what I had done. I hesitated but I had to tell on myself before the knock on the door did. At twelve-years-old, I was terrified of the consequences. When the two cops appeared in the driveway to the house, I met them halfway. I tried to tell them I was alright and that I shouldn't have called. They didn't believe me. It was probably hard for them to believe me as I recounted the mantra that I had come to master all too well, "I'm okay," with tears streaming down my face.

My thoughts ran rampant as the officers spoke briefly with my siblings and parent, asking them questions about my home-life conditions. "Would I be arrested? Would my father be arrested? Would my father be questioned? Would I be removed from my home? What would happen? How did this happen? Why did I do it? Why did I think making the stupid call would fix anything?!" I was scared that I was in trouble and there was no way my father would let me off the hook for the impulsive decision I made. Surely, I was going to be punished. I was most concerned about being punished when I saw the patrol car.

The cops insisted I got in the car so they could take me to the hospital. Though not forcefully, they didn't give me another option. I didn't want to get in the car because I didn't know where they would be taking me. I had never had a reason to visit a hospital in America. I thought about Ma and how much I needed her in that moment. I felt alone and abandoned. The officers persisted. They wanted to take me to the hospital to have me checked out. After their persuasion, I listened and did as I was told. I got in the patrol car alone. I entered the backseat with tears still falling down my face. I was told that my family would meet us there.

Though it felt longer, the fifteen-minute drive to the hospital did very little to calm me down so I was eager to get out of the patrol car when it stopped. I was still crying. I was told repeatedly by the cops and nurses to calm down and that everything was okay. I remember the tears falling even harder as they placed and strapped me to the hospital bed then wheeled me through the ER. The tears continued to fall. They would not stop falling. Tears from fear, guilt, anger, and sadness finally spilled over that day. I couldn't undo the 9-1-1 call.

While strapped down on the moving bed, I thought about my father and how mad he probably was at me.

I was admitted to the hospital and placed on suicidal watch. Somehow, peace came from laying alone in a hospital bed. As the days went by, I was questioned by the cops, the doctor, the nurse, and the mental health specialist. The fear went away, and the anxiety slowly lifted. At the hospital, I was comforted by people who wanted to hear me and people who showed their concern about my well-being. Laying undisturbed in a hospital bed under suicidal watch was the freest I felt since I came to America.

During the hospital stay, I realized that I was no longer daddy's little girl who just wanted to be with her father. Rather, I was the youngest child of a no-nonsense rigid parent. I was the daughter who feared and nearly despised her father and the confining Yoruba culture he ruled his household with. It was becoming easy to hate my father for what and who I thought he had become. In that season, I sadly embraced the truth that somewhere between setting foot on America soil and setting my foot back in my father's house after my hospital stay, childhood died. I was not the same. There was no longer much to smile or really be happy about. A mild depression sat alongside my insomnia.

After my discharge, the hospital mandated that I saw a therapist.

In therapy, even talking was different as I experienced being talked to rather than being talked at. I was the youngest of four at home, so ultimately, I did what I was told when anyone told me to do it. Whether I wanted to or not was rarely ever up for discussion. Besides, my siblings and I rarely conversed much with each other about individual personal matters. Since we were each so busy forging our new lives under the watch of a father who worked three jobs and was rarely available to be a present voice of comfort or warmth, it was easy to accept the unfulfilled bonds of my new life.

CHAPTER 6

Blurry Visions

WHEN I TURNED THIRTEEN, I wanted attention from boys. I saved about ten dollars each week from my lunch money and used whatever accumulated every couple of months to buy new shirts or accessories. A young independence shaved away particles of the little girl that left her mother behind in Nigeria.

I was not allowed to have friends over. I was shy about inviting anyone into your basement home anyway. Even though I was involved in a few extra-curricular activities, the bonds of friendship stopped when it was time to go home. Heeding my father's warning of watching the company I kept, I made sure to always keep a safe distance between me and those who were kind enough to be seen with the African girl.

When the eighth-grade dance came up, I refused to miss yet another dressy event because I had no clothes to wear or someone to make me look pretty for it. I wanted this event to be different.

After saving my lunch money for a few weeks, I asked my father for fifty dollars. I walked forty-five minutes to a quaint clothing boutique that harbored a lovely and affordable pink dress and I purchased it. My excitement trumped the ache in my legs as I walked the forty-five minutes back home.

On the night of the dance, I wore my attire proudly, parted my hair as straight as I could in half, and used black little rubber bands to tie a medium knot. I then rolled the front half left under and pinned it down. Ten handfuls of gel later, I was ready for the ball!

At the dance, I did not miss the stares and whispers as to why my hair was not done professionally or why I had a minimal amount of make up to cover up the minor acne and blemishes that had begun to develop on my face. The disapproval from some of my peers was expected so I endured murmurs and hushed tones of naysayers and continued my mission to enjoy the night. I succeeded. My exterior had begun to build thicker, stronger, and less penetrable. My mother was not presently involved in my development into a woman and I accepted it. I cried less and focused more on who or what to emulate to keep my head held high while in school.

At fourteen, life moved faster, and I tried to keep up. Friendships that led me away from my early beginnings in the church were now secured with loyalty that lacked wisdom and honesty. I think it was challenging to make much room for too many girlfriends in my life because I was waiting on my mother's direction on the right kind of friends. My wait ended after four years of living in America without Ma.

The week of my Ma's arrival, I wondered how joyous the moment would be to have her arms wrapped around me again. I imagined the long nights we would both sit up while she begged to know all that she had been absent for in the last five years. I dreamed about tagging along with her to go shopping for her new wardrobe or getting our nails and hair done together. I imagined many moments in my young mind that didn't make it into reality.

Ma's huge grin was no match for mine at the airport. I locked my arms wildly around her waist and stayed there in her embrace. My mother was finally here and I felt complete in that moment. I felt like the happiest girl in the world to see her again after all this time. Ma's short frame remained the same. Her chubby cheeks and high cheek bones glowed in the airport lights and I clung to her hand as I walked with her and the rest of the family toward the airport exit. It was a great day.

Few months after the joy of Ma coming to America dialed

down, harsh truths set in. I didn't know my mother and she no longer recognized me. I was a girl now searching for validation and comfort outside the cultural confinement of my home. I spoke often but my mother couldn't comprehend my American language and mannerisms. She looked at me often, but it felt as though she couldn't see me. It felt like we both lost our dreams of one another. I expected Ma to be consumed with getting to know me again and falling into place as my mother here in America. She expected me to be submissive without question or ideas of my own and oblige to the Yoruba customs I grew up in back in Nigeria. Neither of us rose up to the other's expectations. As time passed, hope dwindled and I soon attached my love to the honor that I owed my mother. I wanted to be able to give a deeper love freely, but our unfamiliarity hindered that. Indeed, we lived under the same roof, but it felt as though my mother and I were still thousands of miles apart. I had gotten used to life without her presence and the walls grew between us.

At sixteen, I was more concerned about buying better clothes, getting my hair and nails done, and fitting in, than I was about satisfying my mother. I didn't want to need her attention nor strive to meet her expectations. I didn't know then that the attention I craved from others could never fill the emptiness where my love for God and my comfort in God was supposed to be. Still, I yearned to fit in somewhere.

My mother never asked me about me. She never asked me to tell her about myself, but I assumed and silently hoped that she was watching closely. I was wrong. She didn't know my passions or peeves nor could she ever really tell if I was sad, happy, content, or confused about life. Although Ma never stopped being a mother because she cooked and often catered to her family in the preparation of meals and household appearances. It felt like somewhere along the way through the times of our separation and after our reunion, my mother stopped being Ma to me.

To her hesitancy, I set out into the working world at sixteen.

CHAPTER 7

The Church

I GREW UP IN THE Nigerian church that my mother and father grew up in. Harbored in a gated compound, the church was the haven I learned to call home while in Nigeria. The white iron gate was headed by a blue and white sign with the church's name. The sign was complemented by a molded art of two angels with harps, each one flying at the respective ends on both sides of the sign. In English, my church's name is translated as, "Grace." I was raised in Grace, I grew up in Grace, and I learned of God in this church named Grace.

The church was my home. It was a place I resided most often and a place that contained the village that helped raise me.

The church was also the most dysfunctional family one can imagine. Just about everyone was a generation that evolved from a previous generation of devout worshipers. My church was a family of families. Often, members knew more than one's position and gossiped about it to those who did not already know. Nothing ever remained hidden for too long as decided by the church family. Visitors were often found out as quickly as they walked in because faces were that familiar. My father and mother were both influential members of our church home and were highly respected in their rankings.

Being the child of two elders, several church members, many of whom I did not really know, felt compelled to speak to me and treat me with a familiarity that I did not completely embrace. There was an undertone that assumed a role I should play as the youngest daughter of a religious leader. It was presumed that I ought to act and behave distinctively proper seeing as my father was a man of the pulpit. This was a confining platform that my young mind started fighting as soon as it could.

After my father's trip abroad, my mother would bundle all three of us, Mayus, Mike, and I, and we would head to the church for our week-long or even month-long stay. I did not understand every detail but there was always an urgency in the air when my mother packed our clothes and foods and we headed to church. It was not until a couple of years into the exercise of going back and forth that I realized that the church was where my mother felt her children were safest. Fortunately for us, there was a family who lived in the quaint house within the church grounds, so the doors of the church were always open.

Consequently, the church was a dwelling place. The church was also closer to our school, so it helped for the daily commute. At the church, they knew us to be the family of the man who was granted a visa for the Unites States and the family who was always at the church. It was at the church that I learned that anything that had to do with God was sacred. Since the Yoruba culture was heavily intertwined with the church's doctrines of Christianity, cultural rules and regulations aimed to uphold just how sacred the church was. So much so, that it was hard to separate culture and Christianity.

Women covered their heads on church grounds. Women and children were not allowed inside the altar at the church. Shoes were not worn inside the church. Sitting for men and women were separated in the church, as was most other functions to uphold the separation of role and purpose in the house of God. During our church events and anniversary celebrations, only the women were responsible for cooking and serving the meals. Food could not be eaten in the church. A woman could not enter the church during her cycle. A woman could not play the drum or heavy music equipment such as the piano. And the list continued. These traditions were believed to uphold the order of God so there was no reason to disobey them.

I learned to be quiet in the church. I learned to feel the presence of God through the silence at the church. I learned to think purely at the church. I learned to sing in the choir in the church. Although I did not always want to sing in the choir or participate in church plays and presentations, the Yoruba code of conduct regulated a child's behavior in the church. Any adult could give you a directive and you were expected to follow without questions or complaints. Aside from regular school, my church life was another type of schooling. Friendships outside the church were limited and outings rarely took place outside the church. I knew to love the church even before I knew myself, so it was easy to become a reflection of my Nigerian church in its cultural beliefs and expressions of God, which was not always inclusive of other cultures. A gray area stared at me with many question marks.

That gray area questioned tradition and the confinement I felt in the church. Yoruba culture mandated, ordered, delegated, reprimanded, scolded, admonished, disciplined, commanded, and required of me. But the culture did not teach me who God was. Church told me about God, ordered me to worship God, demanded that I honored God, but church did not show me what knowing God and being of God looked like because the ones who held the religious rods of authority evidently often fell short of remaining in the image of God. The hypocrisy, baseless chatter, and proud looks in the church did not look like the God I was taught about. The individual lives and characters of those who assumed roles of leadership also did not always align with God's own principles. The gray area grew.

That gray area stirred up the what ifs on the inside. "What if I didn't agree?" "What if I didn't trust tradition and common belief?" "What if there was another way?" "What if God did not belong in the box that church protected?"

As unsettling as it was, I couldn't ignore the distinct dissonance and resentment against the authority of the church. It remained buried all the way to America until it was called to life by a new church.

CHAPTER 8

Whose Church Is It?

WHEN I FIRST VISITED THE church in America, the sense of familiarity hugged and tugged at my spirit. On one hand, it felt good to be in an environment of people with the same culture. On the other hand, I had the task of embracing a new church family. Here was this little place not too far from the ocean, that presented a promise for worship and guidance. Aside from the chaotic streets nearby, this church soon resembled the church family back in Nigeria in its own style of chaos.

It didn't take long to become keen to the violent streets of Queens, NY. As the months passed, I learned that stories of gang activities, robberies, and fatal shootings were the norm. Yet, the house of God stood unmoved. In the many nights of overnight worship and prayer, the evil never made its way to the doorstep of the church. God covered us. It was the trouble within the walls of God's house that worried me.

With each Sunday came a new elderly face that presumed we would share an intimate encounter because of our similar cultural background. There were no bounds that protected the privacy of a ten-year-old. Every woman assumed a role of mothership and authority that I was reluctant to embrace. Once, an older woman in the church admonished my shyness and counted it as disrespect. She scolded me for being quiet rather than greeting her when I saw her, as that was the Yoruba culture – you always greet your elders whenever you saw them. Whether they were strangers to you was not a factor, you were taught to always show courtesy and respect in the form of a greeting.

Not only was I thrust into a foreign education system with a foreign English dialect, I also felt shoved into a playground with more religious rules and regulations than I could fathom or adhere to. A facet of Yoruba culture necessitated serving God actively by, "doing something for God," in the church. That was the traditional form of discipline in the church. Young girls are automatically placed in the choir section or ordered with brooms in their hands to sweep and maintain the cleanliness of the church. Often, the young boys and young men were directed to mirror the elders in service leadership as they too were expected to lead the service program as early as their teens.

It seemed like it didn't really matter what a child could do well or really wanted to do for God, a child did what he or she was told to do. I saw how this way of worship limited the spiritual interest and growth of many young members. I also witnessed how the limitations placed on who could serve God and how, deterred the progress of the church. For example, most of the young men couldn't play the drums. If only one drummer showed up to choir practice, only one drummer knew the program for the upcoming service. If that one drummer is unable to show up either on time, or at all for Sunday service, there was a disruption in the planned program, where one person was taught and highlighted than others. This left little room for more people to be equipped to do tasks related to any given service. This was the pattern for several organizations in the church and it remained so for too long. Abilities were overlooked and too much power, influence, and attention were concentrated on distinct individuals, so much so, that many felt inadequate and useless in the house of God.

Then came the emphasis on spiritual development at the church. Never mind that it was God's choice alone to choose whom He will use and when, it was common belief that you ought to show yourself worthy to be used in the house of God by how you clap, stomp, and shout your way to the front of the line to be used spiritually. The failure to do what everyone else did during a shout-and-praise session was never unnoticed or without criticism.

My resentment stirred.

In the pronounced creed of the church, your spiritual gifts must be publicly displayed for the world to see, otherwise it is religiously disputed and discounted. My dissonance grew.

I knew I was molded by a religion that I did not accept fully. I often felt that dissonance in my spirit when I chose to love rather than judge. The culture of my church often portrayed non-Christians as sinners who refused to be saved. Outside the church, I felt a willingness and strong passion to share in the misunderstanding of others rather than shun their way of life because it differed from mine. I had friends who didn't attend church, friends whose Sabbath and holy day was a Saturday, and friends who were not raised to know the existence, let alone the power of God. My young core was opened to all persons no matter what the teachings of my religion authorized, and this conflict was uncomfortable.

Although a line of separation grew thicker between my church life and my *real* life, I longed to be a vessel for the Lord. I wanted God to use me. Since I witnessed the power of God through seasoned believers around me, I too longed to share in the glory that God bestowed. I wanted to be able to prophesy into the lives of others through God's messages and be lifted in the higher realms of tongue-speaking and spiritual sight. I wanted to be what the Yoruba church referred to as a *visionary* and a *spiritual warrior*. I wanted to see the battles that raged in the spiritual realms and fight them with the power of God.

Underneath these desires, laid a thirst for the honor and admiration that came with being used by the Spirit of God to become a trustworthy messenger for His people. I observed the acclamation and celebration of spiritualists and I wanted to be celebrated. Pride and puffed intentions concerning service to God encouraged my seeking of God's touch.

Inevitably, I submitted to the moldings of the church. I learned absolute fasting for consecutive days. No food, no water, just prayer for half the day and a meal for each day. First it was three days, then seven days, then fourteen days. The willingness to earn God's selection was deeply rooted. I learned to be still and stand for hours at a time during prophetic hours of the service. I learned to be moved by the presence of the Spirit through worship songs, consistent engagement with the Bible, and the spoken word of God. I learned to pray and know which Psalm to use in prayer against something or for it. I learned the way to be used by God according to my church but never learned to know the God I was chasing after. Resentment, dissonance, and displacement soon melted away in my early spirit as I fervently prayed to be planted firmly by God to do His work.

God answered.

I was thirteen years old when I first felt the intensity of the Holy Spirit. The stillness in my senses of what I formerly acknowledged as the presence of God now moved my being. I moved feverishly against walls and standing bodies as my body shook without control. The experience changed everything I knew about self-control. I now understood why I was trained to be like a soldier in the spirit. Endless hours of standing while praying helped me to be firm and patient as I awaited my turn to deliver God's word. Learning to shout in praise prepared me for the thunderous sound that would erupt out of my lungs when delivering a word of God in tongues. Learning to see food and not care for it gave me the tolerance I needed to sacrifice feeding the flesh for the cause of God in times of fasting and consecration. I began to feel valued by God in another way. I was yet to mature in the wisdom that told me that God valued me even before He formed me in my mother's womb, and this was only a manifestation of the gifts that was freely bestowed to me.

As my spiritual identity formed, I perceived more. The gossips of some church members became louder as I saw and heard things from a divine realm. I heard the whispers among frustrated worshipers who felt the church was not being led properly. I began to see the faults of the leaders and spiritual mentors I had come to trust and follow. I saw their deceit and pride. I saw their arrogance and disobedience. I saw their ways in the light of God's word as much as my young eyes could fathom. Then came the spiritual competition as church members compared the anointing of one to another. I would often overhear conversations about whose spiritual stamina was stronger or whose voice of prophesy was better or preferable.

I watched the beginning and evolution of strife among God's people and saw how a tug for influence and power became a dominant spirit in the church. Many wanted to lead but none wanted to serve. And if they served, they wanted to be recognized properly for their service. Often, I had to remind myself that this was a house of God and not a tabernacle of man. I was compelled to withdraw slowly from individuals that I had come to see in a different light. We all wore white garments on Sundays, but hearts that I believed were supposed to be pure, were rather malicious and dangerous. No one could be trusted. People would smile at you this Sunday and greet you with pretentious warmth but soon gossip about you the following Wednesday to anyone who would hear. I drew in and away from the attitudes that defiled my spirit. I soon felt myself become a recluse. I wanted to protect my growing spirit as a tool of God's work so I stayed away from the spirits I feared may pollute it.

There remained the pressure to display your gifts of the spirit to prove how worthy you were. I had not yet understood that it was never earned because the grace of God through His Spirit was not received by works. Nothing greater deterred my joy in church than the pressure that was placed on me as a spiritualist. During worship times, in moments of undisciplined passion by those who wanted to hear from God, visionary and seers, were often physically shoved in the center of the church and encouraged to go into spirit so they could prophesy into the lives of members. I quickly grew tired serving as a messenger of God. I soon grew weary of church physically and spiritually as I felt my peace shrivel each time, I was called on to serve the people in spirit. I was angered by the shoving and discouraged by the lack of one accord all around.

It was evident that many came only to get their piece of God but very few brought their whole hearts to come worship God without having to receive a direct prophecy. The direction of worship gradually changed. Indeed, many still came to the church to worship. They just stopped coming to worship God. They now worshiped each other.

"Who is singing?" "Who is preaching?" "Who is prophesying?" "Who is leading the service?" "Who is celebrating a prayer answered?" "Who is giving a testimony?" "Who is in attendance?"

These were the prevalent inquiries of many. Less people considered how the church would be cleaned or whether we were all praying for one another as one body in Christ. Less people came to church to celebrate God. Less people came to church to intercede for the nations. Less people came to church to be purified in their body, mind, and spirit.

Having sat back long enough as a witness, I felt the dissonance stirred back up again. Inwardly, I began to wonder if there was still room for God. Judging by the miracles that fell from heaven, there was. Fatal sicknesses were healed. Strongholds were broken. Prayers went up and blessings came down. Many families who sought God for favor in obtaining their American citizenship praised God for taking over the process and bringing their requests to fruition. One couple who had been married for several years without children gave great praise to the Lord for not putting their hope to shame.

Indeed, the promises of God came to pass, and God remained faithful to His church even as a lack of forgiveness and love tore the church body apart. In time, disagreements and misunderstandings between several members on differing opinions became too public too soon, leaving too wide a gap for forgiveness nor reconciliation. Grudges grew and malice spread. It was as though the Spirit of love was pushed out the door and left the door ajar for everything else to come in. Hate, evil, deception, backbiting, gossip, contention, adultery, rumors, disharmony, discontent, and discord daily floated in the air at the church.

The church that had once grew in multitudes from members spreading the good news of God's wonders, now dwindled in number in front of my eyes. Week by week, month by month, less people bothered to show up for Sunday service as more of them walked away from their roles in the house of God. Some opted for the Wednesday night prayer service without obligation. They still wanted to receive but were no longer willing to give more than others to get from God. And even still, the great power of God remained in His house. Admittedly, the church no longer felt like a haven for me. The dissension in my young heart soon made room for a love without the guidance of God or the church.

PART THREE
DETOURS

CHAPTER 9

Crooked Paths

THERE WAS AN AURA OF magnitude about him. Blue was special. We shared two classes together. His smile was gentle and sincere, so it was easy to become acquainted with him. Blue often made it to class late but his presence could not be missed.

Something about the gentle pain in Blue's eyes when he recounted his experiences in life made me want to be there for him. We talked for hours till the sun went down. We laughed freely and fell deeper in the arms of innocent companionship. He was protective. He wasn't too talkative or particularly outgoing, but he seemed to be a friend to everyone. He listened and smiled more to others than he spoke. At times when he walked me home, he often looked around to remain aware. I found out later that he had his own demons in hiding. There were no dates or intentional outings to nurture our closeness, just talking. We talked to each other and with each other, and we listened to each other. We preferred talking in person than on the phone. Something about the honesty in the atmosphere drew us closer by the end of each passing day. We talked about the events of our day while at school or while we sat outside on my front porch. We laughed about characters on TV or spoke about our favorite and despised subjects. It was enough. Blue was a companion that was cherished and wanted, and our friendship was built with an honesty that was needed and protected.

It was enough. But it did not remain that way. Five months later, I got bold enough to kiss him. He had walked me home as usual this night and I wanted to show my gratitude in another way. After the slight peck, he said, "thank you."Blue asked me to be his girlfriend a few weeks after we shared our first kiss. After spending more time with one another, the pecks on the lips became deeper, more meaningful kisses that made my heart race. My body tingled all over at his closeness and I trembled each time. I never felt anything like it. The feelings overwhelmed the skin I was in. It was like pleasure mixed with great fear and eagerness.

I knew I was disobedient in subtle ways to the voice within that admonished me every time I let Blue get too close. Every time I got carried away by kisses and warm touches, I felt a subtle warning in my core. No matter what I told myself before or after those close encounters, my inner man always said its share too. And it disciplined me for a year. A year of restraint and resolve kept me from letting my heart, body, and mind fall into the alluring temptation of what seemed very much like love. Blue was honest about his desires, but he seemingly respected my wishes of a non-consummated romantic relationship between us.

Infidelity soon found its way into our young commitment.

The first time Blue was unfaithful was six months into our relationship. An older girl he met at his job made her intentions toward him known. In our honest friendly love, he told me about it. But then something changed in the way he began talking about her. I heard her name more often than I was comfortable with. A story that began with the events of his day at work somehow always ventured to a story about her. I soon discovered that Blue's body wanted what another was willing to give him freely and Blue wanted to please his body. I told him to get out of his commitment with me. I told him I understood his desire and because of the true love I felt growing in my heart, the bonds of commitment were loosened.

In our time of separation, we stayed in contact and talked still as friends. So much so that he shared his growing urges about this older lady with me. He had an itch and it was not going anywhere until.

She would be his first. He took that away from me. I never lingered on the pain of what I knew would cut deeper than I could ever truly express. I wanted badly for the both of us to honor each other in that way. But Blue's body evidently convinced him that the honor should be given to another, a stranger with a willingness.

My young heart broke slowly in the passing days as I prepared myself for seeing Blue in another light. If we are to get back together, I would have to face that I was still the virgin in the relationship and that shifted things whether I wanted to admit it or not. I was surprised when Blue shared that he didn't go through with it with her. He said that he wanted what he was building with me more. He wanted to share that experience with me, he said. I was elated by his restraint and his place in my heart grew even more. I adored him more for his loyalty to what we were building. Young hearts can be very fragile. And feeble.

Blue slept with the girl at the job about a week later. It happened in the backseat of her car.

I had never known that kind of pain in my life. I know now that the chaotic pulling and discomfort within my chest had to have been the breaking of the bond we built. I had never trusted any man before Blue. I never had a reason to. First, he lied about how far he went with the girl the night before. After I pressed on relentlessly, urging him to be completely honest about what really happened, he finally came clean and spoke the awful truth. She was his first after-all. The news crushed my spirit in many ways. And at seventeen, the loss of place was indescribable. I had envisioned that we would be each other's first. I thought that was my place. I hoped it was. I had begun praying to God that we would make it to marriage and do things the right way no matter how hard it was.

I was plagued by the heart-breaking questions that would not go away nor heal the pain of feeling betrayed. "Didn't Blue understand that the two of us saving ourselves for each other was worth so much more than the momentary pleasure from a stranger?" "Didn't he understand that things could never be the same between us?" "How could we ever connect in innocence again?"

It felt like Blue killed the most sacred part of us that day after Christmas. His unfaithfulness with the girl at the job was the first of many.

Long and painful days of heartbreak and disappointment quickly became weeks of learning forgiveness and trying to move on. I was convinced that there was something worth fighting for between us. I was convinced of the need for forgiveness regardless of how much it broke my heart that he shared himself that way with another even before me while he was committed to me. I gathered in this time that the curiosity within him was over and he wanted to continue building us. The feebleness of a young heart can be dangerous. No one told me then that what was broken could never be tied back together again. I didn't know that the seed of doubt for the future had already been planted. I didn't know that trust was forever lost and if there was any time to walk away from Blue, it should have been after the first time he showed me the kind of young man he was and the one he was not.

Often, we forget that becoming is a process that is not independent of present conditions. I saw the seed of love and strength in Blue, but I ignored the fruits that didn't come from those seeds. I ignored the lack of self-control, the lack of discipline, and the lack of highest honor that Blue was first supposed to find in himself before he could share it with me. I was convinced that at eighteen, Blue was surely aware of what he first needed to nourish within himself, so he did not need me to remind him of the importance of truth and loyalty in an intimate relationship. I know now that I unfairly placed that burden of maturity and wisdom on him because I wanted to be understanding. I wanted to love him past my own pain and disappointment. I wanted to trust that he was a man worthy of my heart and devotion.

I heard my spirit urge me to loosen the bonds of intimacy with Blue completely to be healed and restored without him, but my heart spoke louder, and its deceitful whispers encouraged me to stay. My broken heart won that battle over my spirit. No one told me that a broken heart could never be sound in judgment. I was committed to trying. I feared the pain it would cause me to let go of this feeling of love. So, I decided to embrace the hurt of forgiving him.

After Blue's infidelity the first time, a billion teardrops and many nights of prayer and pain opened my heart enough, or rather tore it apart wide enough till I was convinced to stay. A few billion tears later held me together when I found out about his continued secret sexual encounters with the same girl after their first time. Blue confessed them to me the following New Year's Eve, about a year after it happened. After that, I stopped praying like before. Rather, I adjusted to the pain my heart was getting used to and the tears that came after. But they dried up and I grew up a little more.

Six months after Blue's transgression, my commitment to him became too real. After exactly a year of a tumultuous relationship, I turned a deaf ear to the admonitions of my spirit and gave in to the carnal demands of a worldly love. The spirit still tried to speak through him that day. Blue wanted to stop and wanted me to stop, assuring me that I did not have to go further, and we could wait. Whether it was the anxiety from all that had happened in the previous months or the heat of a fleeting moment, I had already made up my mind in that impetuous state that I was no longer worth waiting for. I just didn't see it.

It happened on a warm morning in June. My junior year in high school was seeing its last days. I felt in my heart what felt like love, honor, and devotion. But I knew it was not nearly enough to warranty giving away the essence that God gave me without God's permission. It was not enough to give away my honor to a man that was not my husband. It didn't take long for me to realize that what I gave was taken for granted and was not cherished for long by the one I gave it to. That day in June, I felt my body turn its back on my spirit.

I knew it was on impulse. Perhaps I got tired of waiting. Perhaps I needed to feel closer to him because of the fleeting trust I felt for him. Perhaps I wanted to rebel for once since being the good girl got me cheated on. Deep down I always knew that this chapter of my life would change me forever.

It was August. I was five days late. I initially ignored some passing nausea in the days passed. But then my brother came home from church on a Wednesday night and spoke to me about the cautionary prophesy that had dominated our church for the last two years. It was a warning to the youth girls about getting pregnant and aborting it. When the forewarnings first erupted in our congregation among the prayer warriors and prophets, I was still a virgin. I dared not consider sharing my body with a man. As curious as I was about the matter, I was terrified of being with a man. But that was two years prior. Now I was indeed in a relationship and I had become dangerously attached both emotionally and spiritually to my partner. But no one knew that because I didn't share the change in me with anyone else.

That night after Mike came home from church with his concerns, something in me rose to attention. I felt inclined to take a pregnancy test. I needed to make sure that I wasn't pregnant. The next morning, I ran quickly to the store to buy several tests. I raced back home and ran into my sister's basement bathroom. I locked the door behind me and took the test. With a racing heart and trembling hands to match, I prayed silently for a negative result. I couldn't allow myself the thought of being pregnant at seventeen right before my senior year in high school. I couldn't be pregnant.

I was pregnant. The test was positive.

Then I took five more to be sure. The second line appeared over and over, and so did the digital reading of the other two that read, "pregnant."

In my first few days of the discovery, I thought about many things. I wondered if this was the beginning of the end. I was the warning. The years of repeated warnings and firm deliveries of church prophesies about avoiding an abortion at all costs, was for me. Those messages were mine. Way before I even thought to sit and listen to a foretelling message, God was speaking to me. I learned then that God's messages are aimed to reach us far before we see the door of temptation we walk into.

After I took the test, I thought to myself, "This could not be my life." "I am now a statistic." "I was a pregnant teenager." "A black pregnant girl at seventeen."

The voices became many in my head. Let's not forget to add in 'the preacher's daughter' title too. My Nigerian culture and beginnings were of no reference. The honors all through my academic career did not factor in. It didn't make a difference that I was an educated young lady who knew of the consequences of unprotected sex. I was purposely ignorant, and I was about to learn the harshest lesson of how costly ignorance can be. The great future ahead of me disappeared in that instant.

These voices were only at the surface of the greater inquiries that pummeled through my brain as the other options poured in my confused mind. I thought long and hard on the situation at hand and considered disobeying God yet again. I questioned the mercy of God if I were to turn away from all I ever believed in and sought a medical solution. I thought surely that God could never forgive my disobedience. This was a life, a seed of life.

"God why me? Lord, why me?" "I have been so good." The voices asked me back, "Oh have you really?"

I secretly pondered what my parents would have to say now. I thought to myself that God was using me as a punishment to their condescending voices about girls who were with child out of wedlock especially at tender ages. What could they possible say now about their own youngest daughter with the best grades and ambitions? I was not so ashamed for myself because this was my first intimate encounter. I was more ashamed for my parents whose good standing in the church community both here and back home in Nigeria, would be tarnished because of me.

I sat helplessly with my back against the bathroom wall. I clutched tightly at my throbbing chest at the thought of my mother bearing the weight of irresponsibility and inattentiveness for her youngest daughter. I wondered if she would feel as doomed as I did sitting alone on the cold bathroom floor on the morning that changed my youth forever.

CHAPTER 10

Bitterness

MY PREGNANCY INTRODUCED ME TO the vulnerable yet cold side of Blue. I never could have imagined it for myself. Without hesitation, he was the first one I called with the heart-breaking news. I wished it was joyous, but it wasn't. The irony couldn't be missed. Never would I have imagined that pregnancy would be heartbreaking for me. When I visited him that morning, eyes puffed and reddened from the tears, he first held me. Then he gently told me that he would support whatever decision I made. I was a junior in high school. He was a recent high school graduate without a job or plan in motion. I was a pastor's child and he was the son of a single mother whose fear of us getting serious too early was now being realized. There was only one logical decision to be made, one that would seemingly make us stronger on the surface, but underneath, strain and eventually break what was left of the bonds of the most intimate friendship I had ever known.

Admittedly, after our last intimate encounter about a week and a half before, Blue admitted that he got carried away and was irresponsible with my body. Blue then suggested that I took a contraceptive pill. The thought of it alone made me nauseous. I was too scared at the thought of what any pill like that would do to my body. I desperately wanted to go all the way back in time to that warm June morning and stop myself from treading on the battlefield

I now limped on. I stood wounded with the startling discovery of my unplanned pregnancy and I prepared to be scarred forever by the pending decision about my future.

When I returned home that morning, I didn't know what was next. Shame and fear moved my feet toward my sister's bedroom door. I confessed everything to Mayus. She first hugged me with warmth and understanding, then told me to wait a few days and retake a test. I never considered that the tests could be wrong. With soothing and knowledgeable words, she somehow spoke a slight hope into my tired heart. There could still be a slight chance that I was not pregnant after-all.

Four days passed, and I took another set of pregnancy test.

I was still pregnant.

The light of hope slowly dimmed, and the tears spilled over even more than they did the first time around. After talking with me, Mayus extended her support to stand by me no matter what I decided. There was an unspoken persuasion to not have the baby, but I know she wanted me to come to the decision without her suggestion. She wanted me to decide what was best for my future.

That night, I prayed earnestly to God for forgiveness. I prayed to be forgiven for my past carelessness, my present hopelessness, and my future disobedience on this matter. Blue and I decided that an abortion was best.

Since the moment I found the clinic's website, I felt the wrestle within. I was about to do something I said I would never ever do, no matter the circumstance. I learned in this season how careless we can be with the word, never. The only time it ought to be used is in admittance that you never know what tomorrow holds. I didn't know how life would or could go on after this. I didn't know how to mask the scar of killing a life that I could not create. I didn't know how I could go on with my life as though this never happened. I didn't know how to play God and get away with it unscathed. I didn't know how I could ever make it to God's house or presence again. Even though I felt like God had turned His back on me, I knew it was me who had my back turned against God. I thought about something going wrong on the operating table. I feared that there would be a complication with the drugs administered. I thought about the clinician cutting the wrong thing. I worried about losing too much blood. The *what ifs* piled in my mind and I feared that the end of my life would be a just punishment for what I was about to do if God saw fit. My disobedience led me here.

A couple of nights before my appointment, I sat by my bedroom door drowning in my tears in the dark. The first punch was light. Then the second time, I punched my lower abdomen slightly harder. Then as the tears poured down my face, I violently punched my stomach repeatedly in the aim of having a self-induced miscarriage rather than going through with the procedure to terminate a pregnancy, as though the intent was not the same. I punched myself harder, over and over, but the pain in my heart stood as tall and unmovable as a mountain so I stopped. This mountain could not be moved nor punched away.

I had a conversation with Mayus the week of my appointment where I half-jokingly suggested another option aside from abortion. I could run away and have my child. I could get a job somewhere. I was smart, I could find a good job and save enough to have my child then come back home. Or never return.

After the words left my mouth, I realized that it wasn't as easy as it sounded. A child needs a home and I was still that child that needed a home. I was set to graduate in the top five percentile of my class. The last three years of advanced classes to attain the scholarship that would get me out and far away from the confinement of home, had led up to this final year. I asked myself if I was willing to give it up for a child that I was not sure I would be able to give my all to. Besides, a baby needed its father and mother. I knew that much. A child needed to be bred in the comforts of love and kindness. In the shakiness of my relationship with Blue, I didn't have the heart for love or kindness to offer myself or anyone else. I couldn't rob my child this way. My young heart and spirit fought gravely with one another and my heart won the battle again after a tiresome effort. Sadly, I had no room for faith in this matter.

"I only care about you getting it done." I will never forget the coldest words Blue said to me in the most vulnerable time of my life. We were arguing on the phone the day before my procedure. Blue was not too concerned about being present for the abortion. He said he would give me the money since the private clinic I chose did not accept insurance. Since I was under my parent's insurance, I couldn't have dared to use it either way. I understood that Blue wasn't ready to be a father. I understood why he didn't want the baby. But we crossed that threshold together. I wished he understood that I too was stuck between my decision and my dreams for the future.

Blue's new attitude toward me was harsh and callous. I felt the distance between us almost as soon as I told him about the pregnancy, but it was still shocking to see how far apart we grew in the following days. It felt like he shut me out and refused to come into full reality with me. I know Blue understood how significant getting an abortion was to me, but his attitude spoke otherwise. It was hard to confess to him that the pregnancy was a life I didn't ask for but wanted. It was impossible to voice my reluctance about aborting a life I was willing to embrace as God's plan regardless of my disobedience. I thought it would be selfish of me to not consider that this same life would forever alter the course of both of our lives because keeping the baby was not a decision that would affect me alone. That burden felt too heavy to carry for the rest of my life.

I spoke to the seed in me the night before we were to be torn apart. I cried and held on to myself desperately. I pleaded with my seed to forgive me for what I was about to do. All I could do was whimper in tears and apologize because I would never see it grow. I couldn't give it a chance to be watered. Shame covered me as I admitted that I couldn't live with bringing a child into this world with its father's resentment. The world was cold enough. I confessed that I couldn't consider the possibility of looking in the eyes of an innocent child to explain why only one parent had enough room to love it unconditionally. The thoughts in my sinful heart further condemned me and deepened the wound of my transgression against my own self and against God.

Little did I know that even in those desperate moments of introspection that I was walking further into sin. Condemning myself was a sin that I never considered during this season of shame and guilt. Here I was, firmly rooted in the word of God since infancy and when I needed to remember most what Christ did for me on Cavalry, I forgot everything I knew about the mercy, love, and covering of God.

Too many of us, too often, thread the lonely road of darkness and condemnation whenever we feel out of alignment with the word of God. We often justify the rebuke of our souls by considering the wretchedness of our deeds, forgetting that Christ paid the price for it all. His blood covers all our sins even before the thought of those sins were brought to life in our selfish hearts. I had yet to receive the truths that the grace of God told.

On the morning of my abortion, Blue changed his mind and accompanied me to the clinic nestled outside our town. I know now that he escorted me there not to show his love and support, but to make certain that I went through with it. I know he heard the hesitancy and fear in my voice the night before during our argument. As we drove there, my sister, her boyfriend, Blue, and me drove in silence. I felt like I dragged my hesitant spirit along as if we were preparing for a funeral. I knew a part of me was about to die.

When my name was called, my legs felt heavy under me as I walked alone into the procedure room. The bright fluorescent light in the room made me sick. Everything, including the intended calming words of the two nurses and the doctor, became an instant blur. All that replayed in my mind were the warnings from church, the argument with Blue the night before, and the voice of the spirit trying its last attempt to make me turn back around and keep the potential of promise inside me.

But as if hypnotized, my legs moved slowly toward the covered bed that was stationed in the middle of the room. My heartbeats became faster and louder. I laid on the bed as instructed. I couldn't hold back the tears when the doctor's second attempt with the anesthesia failed. My veins refused to give way the first two times.

When the doctor moved away from my left arm to insert the sharp needle the third time into my right arm, my body trembled, and the tears poured. I closed my eyes and began to ask God for forgiveness yet again. It was the last thing I remembered before everything went black. I woke up a little over an hour later and it was done. There was no more pregnancy, just emptiness.

Two weeks earlier, the first words Blue had said to me when I showed him the five positive pregnancy tests I took, was, "I'm here for you whatever you decide to do." I wish I heard what he was not saying then. I wish I heard it when he did not say that we were in it together and that he would be there for whatever I needed. I wish I heard him say that he would not let me go through it alone. When I limped out of the procedure room, I lifted my tear-stained face to see my sister and her partner, but no Blue. I asked my sister where Blue was. She told me that Blue left. Blue had asked my sister's boyfriend to drop him home.

Another blur came over me.

I know he had a family gathering to get to later that afternoon. But I didn't imagine that he would leave me there. The reality of it all slapped me hard and the questions rushed in my mind.

"When exactly did he leave?" "When did he decide he was going to leave?" "Did he know he was going to leave me there all along?" "Or did he decide to leave me because he got tired of waiting while I was in procedure?" When I thought it impossible to have any more tears left to cry, my heart failed me. I couldn't contain the tears that spilled over as my sister escorted me to the car.

Later that night, Blue made his way to my house to talk. I ended things with him. There was no going back nor forward. I could barely look at him. I was ashamed of him. I was ashamed of myself. This was the one I gave myself to and as he stood in front of me that night recounting the times I was not stern enough with his waywardness and disloyalty, I marveled at how tragically wrong I had been about the man I fell in love with. My heart bled along with my body. It was so much blood. I could barely walk properly in the first two days that followed the abortion, but I dragged my body and plastered a smile on my face at my new job.

CHAPTER 11

Broken Promises

BEFORE MY ABORTION, I HAD my own notions about those who went through with it. I was taught to believe that people who supported abortions are careless and irresponsible. I too believed that they were cruel and cold-hearted. I thought they were selfish and impulsive, never once considering their own share of confusion, pain, fear, uncertainty, loneliness or trauma when abortion was the only choice out of an unplanned situation. Whether taught by religion or societal standards, many ideas are reinforced by statistics that challenge our ability to prosper out of a dire situation. I think it's easy to be ignorant of what we don't care to know. I also think we forget to live our lives in relation to one another, girded by the undeniable truth that we all are sinners saved by God's grace regardless of what rule we may have broken or misstep we made in a challenging situation. I believe that too often, many of us fail to consider the wars that rage within each person as they struggle to move on from a wrong that cannot be made right in their power alone.

I knew all along that whatever decision I made after I learned I was pregnant, would remain with me. Whether I nurtured the seed in me to fully grow into its own life or buried it with the help of a doctor, a withering had already begun in me.

After two weeks of barely speaking with one another, Blue interrupted the course of my healing the day he saw me walking past his house to the bus stop. That afternoon on my way to work, I crossed to the other side of the street with the intent of not seeing him nor speaking to him if I did see him. I was unlucky.

He spotted me and called my name. My legs moved faster. I didn't hear him running after me until he grabbed my shoulder to make me stop and listen to his plea. He insisted that he missed me and that he was sorry for hurting me. He wanted me to believe that he would never hurt me again. When I charged forward to walk past him, he blocked my path, hugged me, and lifted me in his arms, holding me tighter than he ever had. Then he asked for the chance to make us work and the chance to make things right again. My resolve weakened faster than I would like to admit because he was the only other person who had an idea of the pain and turmoil that having an abortion did to me. I was alone in my pain physically, but he knew the situation and he knew the fears I held about the decision spiritually. I didn't tell anyone else about it so I think it helped to consider that he would at least be an ear for me in this time.

That week, as we tried to ignite the possibility of what I knew was lost, Blue had some confessions. In the following days, Blue admitted that he had become intimate with a former girlfriend, an exotic dancer he ran into at the strip club. I recalled his giddiness about her after their unexpected encounter weeks before I found out about my pregnancy.

I was tired.

My mind, body, and spirit were spent. Still, I wasn't too tired to give our love another shot. We'd gone through so much already. If there was any chance at all that we could make it work, I needed to know. I was burdened by my devotion to Blue and I couldn't walk away completely. I hoped that we could make it through anything if we could just grow from our carelessness with one another. I knew then that I was willing to forgive Blue for anything. He held a place in my heart that I had no control over.

As scared as I was to consider becoming intimate again with Blue, the fear didn't stop me. It took a while, but it did happened, and my attachment dangerously grew stronger to this young man. I have come to learn that fear isn't always a fruit of the enemy's seed. I think the hint we often sense to be more cautious about a decision can be misrepresented by fear. Yet, that strong instinct may be the attempt of our knowing spirit to guide us away from harm. But in our lack of discernment, we stomp toward the grounds of danger without the armor that the Spirit provides. I was no longer a virgin, but intimacy was still very new to me and this newness was a weakness. I looked to Blue to help me grow in understanding of such affection. I know now that it would serve our hearts better to consider the power we fully surrender when we give ourselves so wholly to others.

I fought myself to continue building with Blue. Shortly after we reconciled, he began corresponding intimately with a new girl. She was a gentle girl he met at the church he was attending at the time. I was initially grateful that Blue was interested in seeking God for himself. I felt encouraged by it for our second chance. Then I got hold of the news about their inappropriate communication. For weeks, he carried on what strongly resembled a courtship with this girl. They went out to the movies, where he admitted to touching her intimately. He was also a constant visitor at her job. The good thing about living in a small town is that someone that knows you, or knows someone who knows you, sees something they were not supposed to see, and it gets back to you. For me, this someone, was my closest girlfriend who happened to work at the same place as the girl.

When she told me about Blue's unfailing visit each weekend to see the girl, I was irate. It was almost unbelievable because I couldn't fathom how or why Blue would even attempt to do such a thing. But I knew Blue. I immediately confronted him about it and demanded that he stop whatever it was that he was doing behind my back or let me go. I could not and would not do it anymore. A light argument later, Blue apologized and promised that he would cut ties with the girl. I chose to believe him. I really wanted to believe him. I needed to believe him.

The following Saturday when I caught Blue and the girl talking closely at the bus station, I went mad. I took my time deciding if

I wanted to walk away and never speak to him again. Three long minutes dared me to walk away forever. I charged toward them instead. I looked away from my lying partner and asked the girl what exactly was going on between the two of them. A God-fearing church girl like I used to be, she was truthful and told me that they had indeed been corresponding intimately in what she thought was a courtship. She told me that she was under the impression, as portrayed by Blue, that we weren't together. She apologized to me and proclaimed her innocence in the whole thing. She adamantly stated that she was not that type of girl and promised to remove herself from the situation.

I was grateful for that. Deep down I knew that my problem was not with her, it was with Blue and his lies.

It was a toxic love. Loving Blue was poisonous. And with every situation we passed through, I became addicted to that merciless toxin. I took in more of it every time I told myself that getting back up from every stumble on this journey with him, meant that he was *the one*. I fought everyone over Blue. I fought the friends who told me to let him go. I fought my sister who begged me to let him go. I fought my brother who fought me with silence to let him go. I even waged war with myself. When the stress of my heavy heart got too overwhelming, when I felt like my hurt was suffocating me, I cut myself.

Prom and graduation came and went as I tried with little help from Blue to strengthen severed ties in our relationship. I was determined and desperate to make him the only man that ever touched me. All the heartache had to be worth it. Our union was meant to last through the storms. It had to. I was convinced that it would last if I held on and learned patience through a painful love. It would all get better. I looked forward to college and the freedom away from home. I looked forward to spending more time with Blue and planned to get my car. We both had our licenses so my having a car would give us more freedom to spend time together and go places away from the neighborhood. I had so many plans about us, for us. Two years in and we still wanted to be a part of each other's lives in the future. That was no ordinary feeling. I thought we'd make it work even though 'we' was really a strong *me*.

Through the many storms, I didn't pay much attention to how far Blue and I lived in faith. We never never prayed together. We didn't go to church together. We didn't even talk about scriptures together. As full as this relationship felt with all the mishaps and strong declarations of love and devotion, it was void of faith and the Spirit of God. I prayed for him and I prayed over our relationship, but our union, or should I say the lack of, was tragically unequal and yoked so forcefully on both ends. Even when I prayed, it was not for God's will to be done, it was for God to make my will be done. When I couldn't pray, I released my pain in the ways I knew how. Whenever we got into a heated argument, and we got into plenty, I often ended up on my knees in my room with the door locked and a box cutter in my hand. It started with light slashes on my arm just to release a little pain. But sometimes, I pressed the sharp object deeper until the blood flowed freely. It was my release and my shameful secret.

I also started drinking often. When my thoughts forced my eyes to stay open at night, I drank, often reaching for a bottle and pouring just enough to make me drowsy. I had a stash of alcohol for when I needed it. During those times, I didn't miss the look of agony and quiet anger in my brother's eyes when I walked around with my head down in the house. I didn't miss the sadness of knowing that the lively girl he knew and loved as his baby sister, was no more. That girl was dead and buried. I was a walking ghost. From midnight arguments at two in the morning, to angry text messages back and forth throughout the following day, my relationship with Blue drained life and peace out of me. I no longer had the energy to smile. I had begun to worship at his altar of futile promises.

I missed church as often as I could because I had not yet forgotten that God did not intervene in my mess. I was still angry at God. Little did I know that I had begun to serve another master; one who was void of wisdom, truth, and mercy. Blue was on my mind when I woke and when I slept. It was always a new temptation to admonish him about. There was always a lie I caught him in and a truth that was always bitter. If it wasn't random explicit texts or pictures from some classmate at his college, it was an old matter that stirred up resentment. Our relationship became a battlefield and every time an argument erupted, it was I who limped away with bruises, re-opened scars, and the heavy weight of regrets.

Those days, I would try to recall how and when we strayed so far from innocence. I would try to figure out how we walked so far away from peace and harmony. I hated the indifference Blue showed about whether our relationship would work out. I knew he felt guilty for the pregnancy and the abortion. I suspected that was why he stayed. I think he was waiting on me to walk away from the relationship if he hurt me enough. I sensed that he didn't want to be the one to say goodbye. I think that he imagined I wasn't strong enough to be left alone after all that had happened and the burden weighed heavily on him. I considered sometimes that a silent resentment had grown within Blue toward me because I needed him to stay to try to honor me. I needed him to cover me. I wanted Blue's words and actions to help heal and comfort me. I wanted what he didn't have because in the end, Blue was not God.

The season changed. Fall came and the year was ending. We were in late October when Facebook announced to me that the newest girl at Blue's job was the one in a relationship with him. It happened a few days after our breakup. This news pushed me past the edge, and I fell fast into oblivion. The aftermath was a wave of shocking revelations and events about the man that Blue had become without my knowledge. Too much chaos transpired in a short time and I couldn't believe that this was my life. From cyber-bullying and stalking, to near altercations at my workplace, it felt like what used to be my private life had been exposed for everyone to see and judge. In November, I learned from the stranger that was now Blue's girlfriend, about my most intimate and vulnerable secrets – my abortion, my suicidal seasons, and my former uncertainty as a virgin. Blue shared them all with her and she made sure I knew it. I finally broke. It was the beginning of the end.

I no longer fought but I remained in the battlefield. As the weeks went by, Blue and I contacted each other occasionally, often at my initiation. We weren't together, but according to Blue, he wasn't fully invested in her and the relationship was more of a title than a commitment. I was vulnerable enough to believe in the chance that he was telling the truth but I was also heart-broken enough to remember that Blue was a liar. Blue confessed that he liked her but she wasn't me, speaking of me with a faint honor and high regard. I later found out that he was lying about many things he told me.

On the midnight of Christmas eve, Blue visited me. He stayed with me till the sun came up. In the midnight hours, we sat and talked deeply about how bad things had gotten between us. He told me he still loved me and saw a future with me. I listened. But I wasn't strong enough to believe him this time. Later that evening, he was with his new girlfriend and her family. I knew he was with her because I called his phone and he didn't answer. That was often his way of telling me that he was with her. After all that he claimed was true earlier that day, I decided that Blue had made a fool of me for the last time. Something in me became possessed and before I knew it, the pain and anger overtook me. It was the final straw.

I couldn't go on one more day. That night, I didn't want to live anymore. I felt a dissolve in me. I didn't care to live anymore because nothing mattered to me anymore. My broken heart was the only reality I saw and felt. I searched for the bottle I knew would be there waiting for me. I drank until I felt my chest burn with fire. I then initiated a conversation with Blue's girlfriend via Messenger. We went back and forth for a little while until I decided to do the unthinkable. I called her phone instead of Blue's. I had her number stored from her earliest attempts to harass me and discredit my relationship with Blue.

I knew I had finally embraced the humiliation and rejection when I called her and asked for Blue. I was at my lowest. I wanted to say goodbye. I wanted to say goodbye to him, but he didn't know that I was also ready to say goodbye to the world. When he came on the phone, he was cold and nonchalant as expected. One would never guess that he was sitting right next to me and speaking tenderly to me just a few hours earlier in the day. He barely spoke but he did listen to what I said. He barely gave any responses and hung up the phone as soon as he could.

So, I called again. And again. And again. And again. I called her number about fifteen times before giving up and accepting that he didn't care at all. Blue made his final choice and it wasn't me. I finally accepted what I should have months before we broke up in October. Blue and I were over. It was really over. Our relationship was dead. I lingered on this sorrowful truth before everything abruptly stopped inside of me. The feelings stopped. The crying stopped. The hurting stopped. The headache stopped. And suicide set in.

I called Blue's girlfriend again and left a suicide message. I let her know that when my body was found the next day, she and Blue would know exactly how I got there. I told her that it no longer mattered to me if they were together because I was finally giving in to the pain that all the lies and malevolence had caused me. She won. When I hung up the phone, I got ready to leave the world.

I didn't care to write a suicide note. I sat up in the dark and patiently waited for my parents to go to sleep. I had the perfect suicide plan and I would carry it out once they slept. I couldn't dishonor them by taking my own life while they were awake in the room next to me.

I waited. So did Grace.

Morning came and I had not killed myself. Sleep overtook me instead. I was intent, set and ready to end it all in the quietest way. I was sure it would work. I was sure I wanted to die. I was sure of it. But I didn't do it. I wasn't sleepy but I did sleep. I questioned how sleep crept into my room and into my being that night. The following day passed by in a flash as I still considered killing myself before the New Year came. It may not have happened on Christmas, but I promised myself that I would go through with it before the year ended. Grace promised too.

When my brother, Mike, got the phone call from Blue's girlfriend two days after Christmas, he didn't know what to do. I think Blue gave it to her from the times I called his phone with Mike's number.

I guess he made her call Mike after hearing my suicide message. I don't know what happened or how it happened, but my brother got a phone call that morning and was shocked to find out how bad the situation had become.

After Mike got the call, he confronted me about it. To defend me, Mayus got into an argument with him. When they started yelling at each other, I ran outside and stood in the middle of the street. I was so tired of noise inside and out. Then my father, who I expected to scold my childish behavior, lovingly called me from the streets and begged me to come into the house so we could talk. Rather than my father and I having a private conversation, Mike called a family meeting.

Grace decided that it was time to tell it all. It was time to save me. It was time for my family to fight for me and with me. It was time for the truth.

For about two hours, my mother, my father, Mayus, Mike, and I locked ourselves in my parent's room while Mayus encouraged me to recount everything that had happened over the course of the past two and a half years in my relationship with Blue. When it came time to speak about the abortion, all I could say was, "I'm sorry." I couldn't talk about it. The words hung in my throat while my sister took over.

After she finished, I explained all the chaos that took place since Blue moved on with a new girl while he made empty promises to me. I had never known freedom like I did that day. I found my voice. I found strength in truth. The hold that secrecy and silent shame loosened, and my eyes was opened to see a family's love unfold. When I expected harsh words of admonishment from my preacher parents, I found support in the arms of a mother and father. I found encouragement and warmth in the eyes of a brother and sister. I found hope in the prayer of my family. I didn't need to die in regret or loneliness over the decisions I made blindly in the illusion of love. All along, I had been fighting a lost cause by myself and I had been digging a hole that secrets and lies wanted to bury me in. I had been fighting on the sinking sand that I built a Godless love on. That day affirmed my young knowledge of telling the truth and surely being set free.

I embraced the newness of love and devotion in my family as I felt a door that was once locked open in my heart. Now that my family knew everything, there was a new surge of strength in me. I didn't have to die to feel peace after all. I learned that day how the enemy can sometimes isolate you in your darkest times so he can pour his deceit into your soul. The enemy will remind you that you are too far from perfect and will convince you that life is worthless, that your promises have been ruled out by your sins, and that you are unworthy of forgiveness and another chance at life. I learned then that when life brings you to your knees and the guilt and shame pierces you in the middle of it, the voice that tells you that you belong in your filth and that you are without a savior or a friend, is the lying voice of the adversary.

But the devil is a liar.

I was willing to give my life away to lies and half-truths. But grace waited to fight for me and remind me Whose I was. I belonged to God. I belonged to a merciful, graceful, forgiving God. I belonged to a God who knew I would stumble before I came into temptation. I belonged to a God who was never going to abandon me in my filth.

We need to feel loved in the world. Surely, we cannot help but love another and often we feel helpless in who we love even when they dishonor the love we so freely give. Even when we don't know what love is, we cannot help but feel helpless and vulnerable when our heart allows others in regardless of our resistance. A heart in lust is often left unguarded to be misguided by the lies and illusions of powers we cannot begin to understand without the grace of God. I wish we didn't so often forget that the only enduring Love that ever was, is, and ever will be is the Love that God defines and impersonated in the person of Christ. Another kind of love cannot stand because it is a passing, vapor love created by a passing, vapor world.

Love is patient, love is kind.
It does not envy, it does not boast, it is not proud.
It does not dishonor others, it is not self-seeking,
it is not easily angered; it keeps no record of wrongs.
Love does not delight in evil but rejoices with the truth.
It always protects, always trusts, always hopes, always
perseveres.
Love never fails.
(I Corinthians 13: 4-8) NIV

I loved Blue as truthful as I could. As sincere as my young eyes could see it, it was not God's perfect love. The love I had for Blue fell short of the most important thing – God's ordinance and direction. It is now that I know that God cannot bless what He didn't ordain as our forever. At times, it seems practical to ask God to bless the love we think we found with others. Our impatience can quietly disregard God's authority to present us with the love He knows we deserve, need, and want in the first place. Surely, we are not God and cannot love ourselves, much less each other, the way God loves us, but I believe that God knowingly prescribed love through His word so we may understand what love is not.

Often, I see sex, loneliness, money, power, envy, greed, jealousy, selfishness, misguidance, and lack of understanding, altogether puff up the love that we may deem pure and perfect in our own eyes. A person can fall dangerously short when they lean alone on their understanding, discounting the wisdom of an All-knowing Father in heaven who alone sees every tear and heartbreak in the matters of the heart. Our minds and hearts can be molded in such rebellion, arrogance, and ignorance, that rather than falling on the unfailing grace of God to bless us with His ordained love, we dive blindly with brokenness, deep into another's heart. I almost drowned in the name of love and the one I so deeply loved, could not save me. I know now that Blue probably did not know how to save me. He was not God.

I believed that the end of my relationship with Blue, was the end of everything pure in me. I was stained, damaged, broken, and scarred. Grace said different but I argued still. It was the grace of God that reminded me five years later that although I had not been strong enough to keep my pregnancy or my virginity, although my faith had not been strong enough to trust God in the trials of my greatest failure and disobedience, my life was still worth fighting for and still worth keeping. Glory was not lost.

But the road ahead to see glory again through the eyes of God was undoubtedly a long one. A disappointed enemy, after realizing that a prevailing thought of suicide was no longer an effective weapon, fashioned a new one, self-destruction.

CHAPTER 12

A House Divided

BEFORE THE DECEMBER MEETING WITH my family, my family life was crumbling.

I learned in the last years of my teenage life that pain will often birth rebellion. As a high school senior, my determination to go to college had very little to do with pursuing higher education and more to do with getting out from my parent's roof, influence, and what I felt was confinement. My young mind adopted that college was freedom. I looked forward to the late nights out with nobody to tell me "NO." I imagined rooming with someone new and getting to know everything about them. I was eager about the future ahead that was painted by my wild ideas of freedom. I day-dreamed about the ease of living my life without the intrusion of parents who insisted on molding me strictly by their traditional principles against all odds.

At eighteen-years-old, I wiped clean the tears of the bonds unfulfilled between myself and my parents. I felt love and honor for them and wished for a long time that the ones I loved and longed to honor, knew more about me and the demons I wrestled with as I headed for the transition that was college life. I was the stellar last child with distinct academic recognition among my peers, graduating top five in a class of over 300 students. But it wasn't enough to have and keep my parents' attention. When my father worked three jobs and my mother was not yet with us in America, I told my eleven-year-old self that it was impractical for me to want any more attention than I was receiving at the time. At fourteen, when my mother joined us in America, I told my eager self to give it sometime for her to adjust to her new surroundings and the changes that a new country and time brought. But at sixteen, when my mother and I still barely had a relationship, I felt the doors close on a bond that should have been resuscitated the moment she came back into my daily life.

By then, I was no longer the timid girl I was at the age of nine. I had cultivated some good and some not-so-good friendships and I was not as interested in showing my mother my school transcripts. At seventeen, when I found myself falling deep into the pit of young love, the desire to be embraced and to feel known by my parents was irrelevant.

I knew my parents loved me. I knew it because they worked hard to provide for our family. But the absence of a relationship with them created a void in my young heart. It felt like we were related but not connected. That void grew wider each time I witnessed the outward affection and close relationship between some parent with their child. I wanted a closeness with my own parents, with my mother especially. I had such big ambitions, ones I knew were greater than me but there was none to share it with. I tried my hardest to fill the emptiness of closeness and validation with how much I studied at school. I tried to be the highlighted best student in all I did hoping that the accolades would make me forget what I lacked at home.

As graduation neared, my parents and I didn't agree on many things. I could try and blame it on adolescence and that confusing stage of questioning or wanting to defy authority but that would be a lie. By the time college peaked its head as a near future, I had lost my virginity, gotten pregnant, gotten an abortion, began cutting myself, began drinking, and had a wide array of diverse acquaintances from work and school that my parents didn't know about or bothered to ask about. I knew students in gangs, some who were drug-dealers, some who were gay, some who were atheists, some who claimed allegiance to the devil, and some who defied every moral rule they came across out of the spirit of youth and freedom. This was my world. The veil of innocence had certainly been ripped off from me and my parents were unaware of all my exposure.

I no longer yearned for them to explain the world before me. Life was here and it shook me. I had grown well accustomed to not having my mother or father's hand to hold on to in my most troubling times, so I let life take its best shot, vowing to stand on whatever principle was necessary to keep going. I forgot that there was still a merciful Father in heaven whose grace remained under my stubborn feet to hold me up even when I deserved to fall on my face.

My father occasionally asked if I had decided what school I wanted to go to because he was mostly concerned about loans. Every conversation about college ended with him urging me to go in the route of my siblings, who remained in state for college. If financial aid couldn't cover it, I was advised to not even look at it. Each conversation left me thinking that my dreams were far too big for the house I lived in and I would have to dream smaller or get out of the house. I knew I had no where to go.

Unending hours of research, uncountable scholarship applications, sleepless nights of college essay revisions, and silent prayers to a God I still wanted to believe in like before, granted me my first acceptance letter into one of the top schools in the nation, University of Washington. As I opened the purple envelope and enclosed letter with hope and uncertainty, I momentarily wished that my parents were there to receive the news with me – good or bad. Tears streamed down my face as I read the congratulatory statement at the beginning of the acceptance letter and the scholarship offer that followed. I basked in solitude in a moment of achievement. There was not a parent in sight to hug, high-five, or even just cry with. It was a fleeting moment of joy.

As grateful as I was for the acceptance from UW, I was offered 75% scholarship and a loan offer since an out-of-state tuition would require me to take out loans. I dreaded the process and the loneliness that would precede it as I recalled how adamant my father had been in his warnings against them. My happiness waned about a future at UW but I was motivated and felt confident about my chances of getting into schools with similar prestige.

Scholarship offers soon came from several institutions but none of them were full ride. I needed a full scholarship to prove to my parents and myself that every late night, extracurricular activity, sacrificed play time and fervent efforts were worth it. I needed to know that a school was willing to bet fully on me even if my parents didn't think it was possible because of the competition for such a slot. If they did believe it was possible, their lack of involvement didn't show it to me. Going to an out-of-state college was going to cost me.

The rejection letters poured in soon after UW's acceptance letter. Stanford said no. University of California - Berkeley said no. Washington University in St. Louis said no. Disappointment slowly set in as I realized that my best option was an in-state college. Time was an obstacle.

By the time I applied to all the City of New York colleges (CUNY) available for my intended program, the deadline for their full-ride scholarships had passed and general financial aid was my only option. My High SAT scores, AP courses taken, extra-curricular-activities-packed high school resume, and a 3.8 GPA was not enough to get me to where I desperately wanted to be, where I felt I deserved to be. I wanted the validation that I stopped trying to receive at home and I still fell short. Still I was comforted in being good enough to be accepted into three out of the four CUNY schools I applied to an decided on Queens College.

When a sense of failure consumes you, that feeling of inadequacy can cause you to discard many dreams all at once no matter how long or how hard you fought to keep them in the past. My season of reassessment about college forced me to move beyond my disappointment and still attempt to reach for something more even if the option in front of me was not what I wanted.

While at Queens College, I tried to remain positive about the future ahead. My motivation for higher education fought to stay alive. To no avail, I attempted to join the acclaimed tennis team. I was rejected within the first fifteen minutes of practice. My skills did not come anywhere close to what was required to be part of the competitive tennis team. Then I tried the nationally acclaimed dance team. I made it to the team but couldn't quite make it on the team. The other girls had many years of practice and discipline with the primary dance style of ballet. After three weeks of body-aching attempts to master an unfamiliar and almost hated art of ballet, I walked away. Too much was going on already. The long and lonely night commutes back home matched the long and lonely days going to a school that was not my first, second, or third choice. Though remnants of hope pushed me through the doors at Queens College, remnants of lingering insecurities pushed me out of the same doors after only one semester.

PART FOUR
Cuts and Bruises

Chapter 13

Uncovered

"Her filthiness clung to her skirts; she did not consider her future. Her fall was astounding; there was none to comfort her." Lamentations 1:9 NIV

I TRANSFERRED TO THE CITY College of New York the following year in the Spring semester. The commute was no less painful than it was at Queens College, but it was far more enjoyable. I was still reeling from heartbreak, but I was lifted by a praying mother who knew the power of God to heal and restore.

I soon bloomed again as a student and as a person with life inside of her. I no longer walked like a ghost or lived like one. There was life to be lived, laughter to be enjoyed, moments ahead to give a deeper meaning to my journey, and dreams to bring to fruition. A new hope was brewing. Seeds of purpose were watered by a new atmosphere with new people and a newer mind. But the weeds of self-destruction and ignorance grew too. My time at CCNY evolved gradually as I trounced daily over the past that threatened to rob me from my present and future.

City College was the beginning of something new and there were so many possibilities and opportunities laid out in front of me. By my second semester at City College, I had become a founder and president of my own dance organization, The Freestyle Dance Club.

I had also entered the ballot to become a student representative in student government. The following semester, I continued to grow my love for tennis and made it this time for CCNY's Division III women varsity tennis team. Things were looking up.

My parents and I communicated more. This time, they listened more, and I talked more. But the weeds around my seeds of promise, also grew more. At school, I warmed up to the idea of making friends again and letting new people close, but not close enough to see my brokenness before I ventured to CCNY. I spoke enough to be noticed but hid myself enough that my wounds and scars could never be seen. I started to walk closer to the audacious lines of invisibility. I began to maneuver my way with this guy and that guy. I promised myself that no man would ever get close to my heart or spirit like Blue.

I tried to pray myself out of loving him, out of hurting as bad as I did, out of hoping for a reunion, out of the webs of memories that cut deep. I just wanted to be. I prayed long and hard enough to receive the idea of healing from God, but I didn't wait long enough to receive the healing that I prayed for. Healing requires forgiving. I couldn't bring myself to forgive the betrayal that left my heart bleeding and my character unrecognizable. I felt like the relationship stole from me and killed the me I knew. It took months before I could accept that my normal no longer included Blue in it. I felt bruised and battered. But since Grace did not give me to death, I figured it wouldn't hurt to listen to Grace when it said that I had to continue life and somehow had to learn to put one foot in front of the other. An end with blue was not the end for me. Those weeds of insecurities however were watered by the cynicism that followed my breakup. I grew into a new person. The praying stopped and the waywardness began.

I was not familiar with promiscuity and was always one who valued privacy and delicacy in the matters of intimacy. But that was the girl before Blue. That was the girl before the pregnancy. That was the girl before the abortion. That was the girl before the abandon. That was the girl before. This new girl was reckless and provocative in her most subtle form. She was confident in the strength of her mask. She could put it on or take it off and no one would notice.

She was invisible. She was convinced that the 'good girl' was dead and gone. She wasn't necessarily bad but her guide to life was now freewill rather than faith. And she was indeed free. She didn't know that there was an evil and a danger to an uncultivated freewill.

Without wisdom, it's all too easy to be misled by freewill. Depending on our own knowledge alone can sometimes be just as detrimental as depending on the knowledge of others with ill intentions. Freewill has a way of making us forget that there is a greater wisdom that we should always seek to possess and lean on. Freewill can cause us to exchange our freedom for the enemy's will. That pompous voice will whisper boldly that you should feel free to say and do anything without fear of consequences. Yes, freewill can strip away our highest thoughts and entice us to dive deep and wicked fast in the lowest pits of sin but I learned the hard way that much like freedom, freewill is never quite free.

The separation from Blue made me free. I felt free to entertain the flattery of another. I was free to open myself to another. I was free to engage in playful banter with another. I was free. I was also free to not be as grounded or discipline in the matters of my heart. I was free to be reckless and inattentive to harmful habits or encounters. I was free to be impulsive. I was free.

The idea of becoming attached to another person, let alone another man, was quickly put to death. In its place, was the principle of becoming untouchable, unreachable, and unattainable. My heart was unavailable, so I did not let anyone waste their time with me. My thought patterns were no longer healthy. I was cynical about everyone. I no longer expected a good thing from anyone I met or anyone who showed interest in getting close to me. I saw every man with cynical and perverted lenses, and I treated every situation with the same diagnosis.

One by one, they came about. One by one, they lied. One by one, I conquered. One by one, I devoured. One by one, my pit of ruin was dug deeper. I never genuinely liked any of the men that I shared myself with after Blue. I didn't care to get to know them. I entered each acquaintance with the expectation of a short-term engagement.

The irony often lies in our conviction that the decisions we make are out of freewill. We never stop to acknowledge that the heavy chains of brokenness, pain, and past disappointments are the greatest catalyst to our impulsive decisions. Who can truly claim to have freely sought-after destruction? We tell ourselves that moving on is the only way to get through the pain, yet we merely move along with the pain and the weight of our sorrows, desperately seeking a place to unload them even for a moment. In this filter, we inadvertently begin to create more painful situations with the seeds of discontent and destruction that are nurtured along the way.

With every passing touch, came a stronger hold on my self-destruction. I tore down my own virtue with every agreement I made to consummate a friendship I knew was not meant to be and could never last. The pleading voice of my spirit was buried under the weight of my waywardness. I lost count of how many times disgust and resentment looked back at me when I dared to question what the girl in the mirror had become. I was not shameless, I just got better at hiding it. I was not flattered nor healed by each encounter as I foolishly hoped. But I couldn't bring myself to completely stop. I was ignorant of how sacred my temple had once been before Blue, once when I held myself in such high regard. It was my special mark that God gave to me as a woman. The voices that now made a home in my head reminded me daily that it was I who gave it away foolishly and the loss of it led to my own decay.

As the words come to address each one of these men, I am not ignorant of the circumstances of each encounter. I believed that I had to submit to the conditions of my youth. I thought things would remain as they were. It is now looking back that I acknowledge the state of each young man. Their individual journeys, struggles, doubts, insecurities, and the false truths that they too battled with all played a part. Perhaps it was a pull to emptiness or the brokenness that brought me close to each of them. Either way, my misery sought company and theirs met mine eagerly. These are my love letters, a note of sincerity to every man whose closeness stripped me little by little of all I thought I had left to give as a woman without honor.

Dear Blue,

You were the first, the only one that truly mattered. You kicked down the door that my spirit was not yet ready to open. Perhaps I unlocked it in naivety and hoped you would open it. You were the one who took my hand and led me to what you thought was love. You didn't know where we were headed or whether you really wanted to go there but you wanted me to trust you. So, I did. You were the one whose temptation took me down a path that led through the darkest nights of my life but led me right back to where you found me, right where grace kept me. You were the friend and the love that was never fully understood but welcomed. I wish you knew how to protect and shield me. You left me open and failed to cover me. You left me open when it was cold and gave others the chance to see my nakedness and vulnerability...but I didn't know then what I know now. Your own strength was an illusion. Perhaps that's why I gave all I could to shield your honor. You were trying to figure it out all on your own. You were not allowed to cry. You were not allowed to wear the goodness of your heart on your sleeve for all to see. You were not allowed to show the good that God placed in you. Your birthing place made it difficult to become that which I saw in you. You had to be what your past made you. But I loved you. I loved what God showed me. Grace gave me the strength to cover you and uncover myself in the process. Still, you are forever loved.

To 'The smile'

Your smile was one of the brightest I had ever seen in my life, like blinding bright lights. And blinding it was. I was blind to the many lies and mischief. I thought I needed that smile. Your smile was forcefully persuasive. The smile was friendlier than the man behind it. It took too long for you to admit that there was already another in your life. I wished your truth was revealed to me sooner. But then you knew. You knew your truth would have been enough to make me leave the smile alone and never look back. I told myself it was okay since I gave a part of me I no longer cherished.

To 'The storyteller'

You opened the door with flattering comments and seemingly deep insight, and I walked in. You proclaimed false truths that made you appear wise. But you hid your lies well in the many stories you told. I told myself that this was me moving on from the wound that refused to heal. You didn't have the power to hurt or disappoint me since I dared not expect anything from you. I taught myself to not expect, that I had no such place of honor to expect. But I wish I knew you were a quiet liar. I wish I knew that your words were just another door further down my path of destruction. My broken mind convinced me that your touch and closeness would heal something. I felt suffocated by the shame that spoke so loudly when I sat or laid beside you. I shared too much even with my clothes on. You never should have known those deeper parts of me. You never should have witnessed what was beneath. A quiet liar knew no truth, so how could you ever understand mine? I wish I turned back before I walked in the door of your many stories. But I don't blame you. You did what I allowed you, as I did what my pain allowed me.

To 'The one who called me beautiful'

I wanted to believe you when you said you wanted something more. We were not strangers. I met you first. So, it should have felt right when I let you peel away the layers. It should not have brought tears to my eyes. But it did. It was painful to face what I was becoming. It was painful to know that I couldn't take back the part of me I just shared yet again. I would rather lay in a cold bed than be comforted by the warmth of my miserable memories. You were delicate with your words but coarse with your touch. You quickly forgot how delicate I needed you to be. But perhaps I needed you to *be yet another cold embrace. Since my heart was no longer able to feel past the pain, the discomfort in your rough touch matched my inner turmoil.*

To 'The calm eyes'
You were unpleasant. You waved dishonor in front of me and I clung to it. My lust with you gave my spirit the most gruesome battle. You were hateful and cruel. You treated me with little compassion and spoke to me like I was dirt. Your crass manner reminded me how little and insignificant I had become even in my own eyes. I believed that you said out loud all I thought of myself. Your maltreatment of what used to be my temple glorified the conviction I now held as what was. Perhaps I was nothing. The places, the actions, the conversations, all shadowed a dying grace within me, a shuddering flame of what used to be my light. I was glad when you said it would be the last time because the one you loved was coming back to town. Then your cold ways finally made sense. I shared too much with you. You betrayed even the slightest illusion of safety that I hoped for.

To 'The greatest misstep'
You only feigned concern. Your sudden interest struck me. You were my greatest misstep of all, my most unforgotten disgrace.

CHAPTER 14

Naked Shame

ALMOST THREE YEARS PASSED BEFORE I allowed a doctor to get close to my most secluded place. The abortion was the first and only time a doctor ever needed to look down there. Now here I laid, a nervous wreck, seeking a diagnosis for something unfamiliar. The female clinician turned her light on and looked closely at the physical symptoms.

"It looks like herpes. I'm pretty certain it's herpes," she said, with all the assurance one could expect from an expert. I remained frozen with my legs in the air. I felt my heart stop beating for about a second. She had just uttered the fear that chased me to her door in the first place. I had finally gone too far. My careless ways had finally dug my inevitable grave. This was it.

It was during the rainy drive home, that I knew what it was like to feel like a wasteland. There was no friend I dared to call. I felt my breathing skip several beats again when I considered having to share another shameful truth with my parents. I couldn't possibly shield them from this. My father was the first option. I would tell him first. But of course, this was a fleeing thought. I wondered if it would destroy him as much as it was destroying me. Fear coursed through me as the raindrops fell hard on my windshield resembling the heavy teardrops that fell from my tired eyes.

The questions started. "How would life change?" "How many pills will I have to start swallowing to live long enough before I got a bad cold?" "Is there hope for having a husband or children?" "Do I even still believe in marriage?"

As I drove with caution in the stormy weather, I thought about my next course of action. I thought about driving into oncoming traffic or calling on a God I was not sure would answer. I continued crying, trying to breathe through the discomfort that lodged itself in my throat. In between my uncontrollable sobs, a familiar voice found its way through my lips and it dared to call on the God that I turned my disobedient back against. Something about being in a place of desperation like never before will cause you to cry out to God like never before. In a voice I didn't know I had, I cried out desperately to God:

"PLEASE. PLEASE GOD... PLEASE GOD... PLEASE GOD... PLEASE OH GOD," was the most I could get out for a while. "PLEASE GOD FORGIVE ME! FORGIVE ME GOD! I KNOW IT'S MY FAULT BUT PLEASE GOD! PLEASE FORGIVE ME FATHER! GIVE ME ANOTHER CHANCE LORD. PLEASE DON'T LET IT BE! PLEASE DON'T LET IT BE! PLEASE GOD DON'T LET IT BE!"

In that loneliest moment of helplessness, humiliation, and remorse, I knew I was begging for my life. I knew I was begging for a chance I didn't deserve. I knew I was begging for mercy that I could never earn. I imagined how devastated others in a similar place must have felt when they first received the news. It didn't matter where you came from or what led to the results, a pain like that was unbearable. I imagined that the burden would weigh as heavy as mine did now. I wanted to disappear. Guilt and shame stifled my breathing again.

As the twenty-minute ride home from the doctor came to an end, I mustered enough control to talk to myself. I concluded that I wouldn't say anything to anyone until I got the official results. The wait began.

It's amazing how grace fights for you even when you dishonor it. In the depths of my broken heart and spirit, I had faith that God could still hearken to my desperate plea. That night as I laid helplessly hopeful in my bed, I made a celibacy vow. It was really a vow of abstinence because I no longer believed in marriage or forever after. If I was honest with myself, I didn't comprehend the weight or grace of celibacy in the environment I was in. I certainly no longer believed that marriage was part of my life's journey. I didn't see myself fitting as somebody's wife nor did I believe in my ability to love again. Once was enough. I promised God in all my feigned humility that if He would hear my cry, that I would no longer indulge in any intimate encounter for a year! No more fornication and vowed a desperate me. I would fight and resist lust if God would give me one more chance to rise above the temptations.

I should have known then just how far I was from God's truth. Here I was at nineteen nearing twenty unable to trust myself with such a vow, not because I lust for a man's touch but because I had grown accustomed to the wasteland that was my virtue. I had no standards nor investments in moral philosophies and psychological jargon about deep connection where sex concerned. I expected some man soon to profess the possibility of something, anything to me, that I most likely would give into if he tried hard enough. My perverse mind was now convinced that I dwelt in a society where giving my body was necessary in the discovery of love or anything that looked like love between two people. I was convinced that there was no escaping it. My foolish sense told me that this was the harsh reality and I needed to stop lying to myself believing otherwise. No one wants to be with a girl who would not get with the program. Sex was sex. It was just that. It was no big deal like I once held, nobody cares about waiting for marriage, and that marriage was a withering custom as most of my peers believed anyway. Judging by the rate of divorce, extra-marital affairs and crimes of passion every day, it made no sense to be hung up on the idea that I was special enough to inspire such patience from a man. There was no bed to lay for such dreams.

None of this mattered now as I waited for the confirmation of the doctor about my test results. These were the longest three days of my life. I dreaded the inevitable call from the doctor and prepared myself for the worst.

On the third day, when the phone rang, I picked it up with my breath held by fear. A solemn calm came over me when the doctor, who had been so sure a few days earlier, now changed her expert statement.

"You are all clear. It wasn't Herpes..." She probably added a few more statements to her report but I momentarily drifted elsewhere while trembling hands kept the phone glued to my ear. The tears slowly fell. God heard me. God really heard my cry. Wretched as I was, disobedient as I was, wicked as I was, God heard me. Faith saved me. Mercy received me.

But I had not yet learned because my love letters continued.

> To 'The supporter'
> We built a friendship long before I started on my path of destruction. You supported me, encouraged me, and inspired me. I think I trusted you the most. Especially after you handed me the keys to your car that one time so willingly. I'll never forget the beauty and warmth of our summer night. Then time turned you cold. And I shiver still at the chill of who you became. But it was too late. You already took what I fought with myself about giving.

> To 'The carefree spirit'
> Knowing you started as a good thing. I needed your carefree spirit. It was a different kind of oxygen, one your carelessness polluted. The way you were with your little girl gave you a truth you didn't even know. I expected more. I had questions you never bothered to ask yourself. Our time was short-seasoned. But I thank you greatly for the laughter you gave. They nourished my soul.

I lived my life as carefully reckless as possible in the matters of my heart, body, and spirit, but inwardly, I longed for rest. I longed for the happiness and peace that continued to elude me. I wanted to stop. I wanted to say no. I wanted to feel more power against this force that told me I was helpless against temptation. But still I stumbled.

Nothing else is powerful enough to halt your race like death. It rarely ever knocks before it comes in. The thought of it alone forces a stillness that cannot be avoided. Something about death, the abrupt ending of a life you knew and loved, the sudden disappearance of a person who shared in your memories and joy, can bring your rapid movements to a halt. Death makes certain that you acknowledge its arrival no matter who you are.

The warmth and brightness of the summer sun on July 7, 2012, was to be remembered. The sun was shining just right, and the summer breeze cooled the air. I was at a friend's barbecue when Mayus called me around four in the afternoon. She was crying and her voice was frantic. She was also three-months pregnant with my nephew. I asked her what was wrong and she told me that Sonny had been shot. I froze with shock and hope as I digested the un-welcomed news.

Sonny and Melisia Evans were like the god-brother and god-sister I never officially had. Melisia started out as just my sister's best friend but our families grew closer over the years. We call her Lisa. I had known Sonny and Lisa since I was eleven. They watched me grow up and we were family. Sonny was the DJ to all our parties and Lisa was the sister that I always wanted and got. Her kindness overflowed whenever we got ready to do something as a family. Lisa contributes with her presence, her cooking, and her hair-styling skills. She was my sister in every way as Sonny was another older brother.

"How did Sonny get shot? Who shot Sonny? Why? Where? How?"

As Mayus tried to explain to me why she was currently on foot making her way to Lisa's house, the shock I felt controlled my forced movements. I got up from the park bench and dropped my burger. My appetite vanished and fear rushed in. I too started walking toward my car. She said Lisa had called her with the news that Sonny had been shot. She didn't know what happened but the thought of losing him was enough to go to the house immediately. I tried to calm her down. I was unable to muster up the courage or faith to tell her that everything was going to be okay. I didn't know if everything would be okay. It didn't feel like it was going to be okay.

Nobody we knew so personally had ever been shot. Nobody I knew had ever been shot and lived to talk about it. But I told her that I would meet her there. I got in my car and drove with a nagging uncertainty. I was brought back to the years of losing my uncles and aunts back in Nigeria. The grave feeling made its way from deep down in my belly and crawled to the top of my lungs. I felt death creep up.

When I made the left turn on Lisa's block, the chaos stretched in the form of cars and siren lights. I parked. I took one breath after another as slowly as I could. It wasn't a good feeling. It felt like a dark cloud had set in. I felt a loss of air as I made my way past the groups of crowds consoling one another. I saw individuals sitting on the sidewalk. I looked up and saw the yellow tape that stretched from around the house to across the street, and then around the tree.

Where was Sonny? I had to see Sonny. Had he been moved to a hospital? Where was he?

Then I heard a familiar sound. The wail of Lisa's mother confirmed the tragedy that had set up house in my throat. She was talking loudly and incoherently while beating on another woman's chest. Then I looked to my right and saw the figure on the ground covered in white cloth. I found Sonny.

I tried again to breathe in and out slowly. After many years, death found my family again. I stepped back from the gate of the house. The red and blue lights blurred my vision for a moment. Then I turned around and saw Mike get out of his car to walk toward me. I had never seen Mike cry until that day. The tears poured out of the both of us as we clung to each other. Sonny was dead. Someone killed my brother. Death took my brother in broad daylight. No explanation sufficed for the questions that ran through my mind. There was only an air of death and confusion. Sonny was gone. He was twenty-six-years-old.

I experienced a shift after Sonny's murder. The world felt colder and scarier. Since his body was to be buried in Jamaica, Sonny's family and friends gathered the following Monday for a memorial by the site of his murder. We had candles and flowers to hold to his picture that was plastered to the tree in front of the house. I couldn't believe that Sonny was dead. I wore a pink tie to the memorial since he always wore ties to most outings. I couldn't contain my emotions as I read these words at his memorial:

> Dear sonny,
> A billion tears could never express the heaviness of my heart since your departure,
> A billion hugs could never replace the one that should be from you
> A billion kisses couldn't give the warmth that a kiss from you would
> The tears are stuck in my chest like heavy boulders
> I cannot get them to fall
> I want to cry and let out the pain and anger of losing you so soon, so violently
> But I can't dear brother.
> But can you tell me this to placate my worries?
> Are you warm up there? Have the angels received you?
> Are you sitting on a long chair with your eyes closed?
> Facing the brightest sun with your cool shades on?
> Or are you doing your thing spinning a record with the angels?
> Are you mixing the music for the heavenly hosts?
> Are you at peace dear brother?
> Is your heart finally empty of weariness?
> I thought and hoped just as much.
> your smile says it all. oh, dear brother, it pains me so greatly to think
> of never seeing you again.
> But I am so joyous because I know you are well.
> You are shining your light up above,

You are sharing your hugs with the angels,
And you're still sending those sweet kisses from the
clouds to the ones who miss and love you so dearly.
God wanted his angel back and we should accept that,
But we will forever wish we had you here for much longer.
We love you so much Sonny.
Please tell God to heal the pain in our broken hearts,
And to let His justice reign here on earth.
Dearest, you are forever in our hearts.

It can be confusing to experience pain and loss amid joy and excitement. Mayus shared the news of her pregnancy a couple of weeks before Sonny's death. Mike, Mayus, and I were also traveling to London for the first time together the following week to visit our cousins. The two of them visited before, but it was my first trip to London, and I was thrilled that we would be there together. Our excitement intermingled with discomfort over Sonny, but we were encouraged to count our blessings even more since we still had each other. The trip meant more now in the wake of admitting how fragile life was.

In London, I mourned Sonny's death in my most private times because I didn't want my sister to see me cry. She was a little over three months into her pregnancy and I didn't want her to worry about me. My mourning evolved as the days passed. I mourned the death of my love and friendship with Blue. I mourned the death of my young faith. I mourned the death of the girl I once was, the girl I once loved, the girl I was once proud of. I mourned the death of the seed that was my pregnancy. I mourned the loss of hope. I mourned the death of my ambitions. Then I cried some more over Sonny's death. I knew it was time to bury my destructive ways. I couldn't go on the same feigning strength and confidence in my suffering.

I knew I had a long way to go to build my faith back but I was ready to start. I was ready to receive healing if God was still merciful enough to grant me even some of it. Overall, the dreary and sullen weather in London matched my melancholy spirit. Still, I committed to enjoying as much of London as I could. I was eager to get back home in the States to find the pieces of my life and beg God to make something out of nothing again.

My love letters continued but they were written slower. I was not okay with being 'okay' anymore. Still I stumbled.

> To 'The artist'
> We had a connection, a bond like no other. We talked as friends and played like family. We played together then you played with my mind. You dishonored my time and made me question all that I thought was becoming right again about me. You kissed me like you knew all my secrets. Then you put me out in the rain the next day. You woke up next to me and called it a mistake. You asked me to leave even though it was still raining. You turned a deaf ear when I professed my love, or the closest thing to it that I could feel. You said I was not a priority, so my love had to wait its turn. I prayed you would regret it. I'm glad you later confessed that you did regret it. It was a sweet confession to hear.

God knew that I no longer recognized what love should look or feel like. So, He started with a new life to teach me. On January 24, 2013, my nephew, Ian, was born.

That January morning, I rushed to the hospital to see the little one I couldn't wait to meet. The joy in my heart was full and overwhelming. Ian was finally here! Here he was, perfect as could be in my arms. I didn't know a love like that until I met him. I immediately felt comfort holding him for the first time. This was new love. I didn't know it at first, but Ian was surely part of my healing. I didn't know then that the late-night cries as he wrestled sleep, and the early morning ones that disrupted my slumber and stirred me up would bless my broken heart from the most painful decision I ever made in my young life.

Time after time, Ian's innocent smile would warm my heart and bring tears to my eyes as I often imagined what the smile of my own child would have looked like. When Ian laughed, his soft sounds filled the room, making less room for my pain. This was a new realm of love. Once, in Ian's first weeks from the hospital, his father asked me if it was too weird to spend so much time with Ian as often as I did. Perhaps he felt or even saw a glimpse of my pain without me knowing. But I assured him that God was healing that part of me too. With this little one, I found my way back to a love that was pure and innocent, one that was given back in small doses whenever he clung tighter to my hand while we played. It took a lot of self-destruction to realize that no matter how deep I attempted to bury my pain; it was never deep enough that it couldn't be dug back up to hurt me all over again. I gave up on God's healing, but it never gave up on me. Though he came into this life as my sister's son, Ian was part of the restoration that God allowed me to see, touch, and hold. My love letters yet continued.

> To 'The unfamiliar one'
> Your boldness caught my attention. No guy had ever invited me to breakfast before class. You said that my focus on my future intrigued you. I was caught aback by your sincerity and the unfamiliarity of all that you represented. You enticed me with your refreshing thoughts and habits. Then the spark disappeared as though it never existed.

> To 'The guarded star'
> I thought for sure I was ruined with you. My eyes were not without tears for long. I thought I owed it to my past to try to love again. You were cruel enough to take the closest thing to your affection away. You would tease me with the idea of love then refuse to talk to me and pretend I was not right in front of you. I was easy to ignore. You assaulted my heart and toyed with my head. It was your favorite game. Since everyone before you had been a different kind of abuse, I allowed yours to be justified. The late-night requests to visit you spoke volumes of the honor I lost long before you. It took too long for me to see the ink of her name on your skin. I never

looked. I did ask if there was another in the beginning, but you lied many times. It was painful to see the history, present, and future of your love on her ring finger. I lost again. But so much was already lost in me. I fought myself for you even though you never once called me yours. You used me then you cast me aside. I tried to convince myself that I allowed it but that was a lie. Your abuse subdued me. It demanded my submission and I obliged. Over and over you lied and I stayed. I should have stayed away.

To 'The last temptation'
My heart was still in shambles when you came around. Although I had run to the altar of grace and forgiveness, I couldn't resist walking into your tempting arms. I wanted you to be a new kind of hope. I should have known that it was too soon and without order. Something about the attention you chose to give, gave me something I never thought I would want again. You referred to me so highly. I thought I saw what resembled honor in your eyes. Then you confessed. You made certain that I knew what we were not. You made certain I didn't think too much of anything we shared. You made certain to remind me that I was your greatest pleasure and that alone made me worthy. I know now that I was supposed to pray for you and lead you to something outside me. Flesh got in the way. You were my last temptation.

By the time college graduation rolled by, the stench of my sexual immorality was not far from me. I wallowed in secret as my disobedience and negligence daily fought to squeeze the goodness out of my life. I tried to be happy and content with the mess I made and the filth I was. Indeed, the world I lived in said it was okay to be as unruly, broken, and rebellious as I needed to be 'to be happy.' So why did my soul feel so heavy with regret and guilt? Why did I feel like a trapped swine in a cage of waste and grime? Why was it so hard to ignore the odor of my sin?

CHAPTER 15

Let the Church Say Amen

AFTER MY ABORTION, I THOUGHT I buried the pain, confusion, hurt, shame, guilt, regret, and sorrow of my misstep. I later learned that they all buried me. My pain buried my laughter. My confusion buried my truth about God and all that church taught me about the Holy Spirit. My hurt and shame buried my confidence in who I was in God. My guilt and regret buried my faith and resurrected a belief in un-forgiveness, so I focused on hiding out.

In those times, the church was the last place I wanted to be. I didn't want to worship at the church out of fear that someone led by the Spirit would see through me and expose my muddy secrets to the whole congregation. I was stained and I felt the cold eyes of shame wherever I went. I truly believed that a gruesome punishment was ahead of me for all I had done, and I believed it would be deserving. I knew my actions were cowardice and wicked, so I hid in my shame. As much as I convicted myself and expected God to turn His back on me or to curse me, I begged and hoped that God would do so in private. I didn't mind the correction as long as no one else could witness it. So, I stayed away from Sunday services and avoided serving at church. I no longer had a heart of worship. Rather, I felt the heartbeats of a wicked sinner, a sinful saint. I felt like I wasn't worthy to be used by God anymore because I was no longer sacred. How could I return to God's House and God's presence to bow at

God's feet and bask in God's glory and holiness when I was no longer pure? How could God look at me and not see the filth, waste, and disgrace that I saw and felt whenever I looked in the mirror? It was unthinkable to compare my numb heart to the heart of the one who once sang and danced about the grace of being clothed in God's majesty.

Many months and heated arguments with my parents passed before I went to church regularly again.

Several months passed and my shaky footing in church proved even more fragile and incapable as a wave of unrest at church was stirred once again. The battle ground for influence and dominance started again. The characters of leadership were in question yet again and this time, things took a turn for the worse as private matters became public and public matters became private. Outbursts during meetings, disagreements over church funds, and other avoidable matters took over. The pillars of trust fell left and right and all around the church. As misunderstanding and mistrust grew, weariness quickly followed. It seemed nobody committed to anything anymore as leaders walked away one by one from their assigned roles. The house of worship was a broken house and being a witness to all this became part of my conviction to keep away from church.

As I saw many more members of the church turn away from a place they once vowed to always remain, the frailty of loyalty broke something in me and I it hurt me more than I wanted to admit. I thought the church was supposed to stand when everything else crumbled. Nothing prepared me for the last straw that caused the last stone to topple over.

During a worship session, while in a trance state, a highly admired and favored young prophet testified against a well-known and respected spiritual leader in the church and declared her a witch. Further proclaiming to be led by the Spirit, the youth accused the spiritual leader of using wicked sorcery to harm the church and its members. As one can imagine, her accusations evoked much chaos and disruption. That night marked the end for many who had been hoping on the mercy of God to revive the prosperity of the church.

The end was indeed near. The church that was once a blooming seed of faith, hope, and prayer, was now a dying tree with withering leaves and branches. About eighteen committed members, including myself, were left after the incident. We all wondered if the church would stand after this. We waited on God.

I turned twenty-one the year after the scandal. That December, the doors of the church were permanently shut. Although the church closed primarily because of a lack of funds, I'm convinced that we lacked more than money. For me, it was not the lack of money, but the abundance of deceit, envy, strife, un-forgiveness, and unfaithfulness, mine included, that caused the church to close its doors. The thought of starting over yet again at another spiritual fold was frightening. It was easier to accept that the church was no longer an anchor. After these doors closed, I folded my white garments and shut the door to my faith being grown in a place of worship. My faith was faintly breathing but church was definitely over.

CHAPTER 16

Mirrors

"Then I passed by and saw you kicking about in your blood,
and as you lay there in your blood, I said to you, "Live!"
Ezekiel 16:6 NIV

THERE IS NOTHING QUITE LIKE an unmoving pain, hurt so deep down in your soul that it takes hold of you and refuses to let go. I thought it was my past that refused to let me go. It took a while for me to see that because I nurtured the strongholds of past disappointments and bad decisions, I was the one who made room for pain to live with me. Pain will cause your mind to receive an act of kindness with suspicion. When a new person comes around, pain will remind you what happened the last time you received someone new with hope and truth. In my pain, I shut the door to others. In my pain, I was distrustful of everyone and refused goodness and kindness from anyone.

After Blue and I ended, I think I held on to that pain. I think somehow along the way I allowed the voices in my head to convince me that my pain was my badge of survival and I was to wear it proudly. I never stayed close enough to God to let go of my pain because I was unwilling to relinquish this badge that allowed me to say that I had been through all that pain. It felt like I was always trying to fight myself out of the comfort of God's hands. Like a stubborn child, I wiggled and wrestled away from God's arms and fell back in the arms of whatever or whoever else I could find that wouldn't force me to uncover my pain.

I rejected healing from God because I knew that I would no longer have an excuse to be shielded by my destructive trail. I was convinced that healing would expose the depths of my brokenness to everyone around me. My vulnerability would have to be uncovered if I sought healing, so it made more sense for me to hold on to the discomfort that gave me a motivation to appear fearless and confident in the eyes of others. Only I knew and felt the demons alive inside me, gnawing at my flesh, puncturing my resolve to appear strong.

I played the heroine part all too well with one young man during the last leg of my undergraduate studies. Let's call him Pisces. Our age difference was only three weeks apart but younger he was still. I could tell almost instantly that our spirits didn't agree with each other. Yet, I told myself that there was room to grow. Never mind that he was as hot-tempered as I was cool-headed. Never mind that he preferred to use his tongue as a sharp sword and I desperately wanted to use mine as a tool of harmony. Opposites attract they say so I allowed the attraction that pulled me into yet another dimension of chaos.

Before Pisces, I never experienced abuse and manipulation with anyone that professed their affection for me. This trial was indeed new to me. I was attached to the relationship long before I realized that it was built on mind games that he played better that I ever could. I may have been good at pretending that I was confident and rid of all my past hurt but I was a horrible liar. Pisces on the other hand, was a skillful tale teller who said things that I easily believed and wanted to believe. Even when I had questions, he would respond in such a calculated way that made me question my own questions.

God is consistent. Man is not. I couldn't ignore the inconsistency and uncertainty in my relationship with Pisces. Yet, I validated them. I was in a place where reasoning solved every problem in sight. The only problem with my reasoning was that it was baseless, and it once again lacked the backing of God's ordinance and wisdom. I got so used to hiding my pain and carrying it well that it convinced me of an immunity that didn't really exist. With Pisces, I fought tirelessly for respect and honor. I hoped that Pisces could somehow help me make sense of who I was. I hoped that I could receive honor and virtue in a place that I was willing to sow in tears again.

For about a year and a half, Pisces came in and out of my life and played on my many weaknesses. With him, I shared my need to fill a void. I shared my desire of wanting a lasting companion. I shared my yearning of wanting any reason to smile. I was vulnerable and he knew it. We ought to be very careful about who we share our vulnerability with because not everyone can handle our nakedness. Pisces occasionally shared personal details of his life that he knew would evoke enough compassion out of me, then he played on my heart strings by testing my loyalty. When he was available, he would make me choose spending time with him as opposed to completing a task or another obligation to see how willing I was to compromise my schedule to fit his. I knew things about him, about his past, his personal struggles and strive. He often used what I knew of him to control how I responded to him, as though a reminder of how honored I should feel to know such depths of his life. No one had to tell me that Pisces was in control of us. When we talked on the phone, when we saw each other privately, or how we engaged with one another in public was all up to him. I had to follow his lead or face being rejected. I had to oblige to his requests or watch him seek another.

During the spring of my last year in college, I had hopes of spending time with Pisces for spring break. Since his declaration of love for the first time earlier in the new year, my doubts about a future with him waned for the umpteenth time. I finally considered building something lasting after all the tumult between us.

I was at dance practice prepping for an upcoming cultural festival. After practice, my friend and I struck up conversation. When she mentioned Pisces, I shrugged off his name nonchalantly. I decided it best to conceal it from everyone until I was sure. He had not even met my family yet. Too much back and forth had gone on between us and I could not yet shake the distinct uncertainty that nagged at me on the inside. As we discussed Pisces casually, my friend asked in curiosity, "Isn't he like engaged to his girl now?"

I froze. "Huh?"

She continued, "Yeah, I peeped him on Instagram all in love and what not."

My oblivious friend passed me her phone and there it was. All of Pisces' lies on a silver platter, including an inked name on his arm. I never looked. I never saw that name. Granted he had more tattoos than I had ever seen up-close in my entire life. Everything else faded as I glared into the facts before me. But how could I have missed it? I didn't want to admit that I might have been blinded by my desperation to build something out of nothing with him. I knew Pisces was sometimes mean-spirited to others unnecessarily, but I concluded that just like me, he had his demons that he battled with. I didn't want to see him the way everyone else did from the outside looking in. I wanted to believe in the gentleness and tenderness he often showed when we were behind closed doors. I could never have imagined that he could lie so truthfully. Pisces made me question my truths to cover his lies. Pisces seemingly shared himself intimately with me but all along withheld his heart at all cost, insisting on blaming my insecurities for not trusting him. I was astonished by how boldly he took from me, all the while knowing what he would never give back.

It took everything in me to control the trembling from within before it reached my hands as I flipped through pictures of Pisces with a girl, I recognized from a couple of his basketball games; a girl I was convinced had to be a younger family member. The photos and videos before me celebrated three years of love and bliss.

"Three years!" screamed the inner me, as I handed the phone back to my still clueless friend. I was determined to show resolve in her presence. She didn't need to know how foolish I had been to believe in Pisces and his lies. I was covered in shame as I considered how cheated I felt by a man that never claimed me as his own in the first place. This time, my heart break was slow and agonizing.

As I drove home with unsteady hands, my heartbeats threatened to pound out of my chest. I tried to force my mind to do what it did best – rationalize. I tried to tell myself that Pisces and I were never officially committed to one another, so I was not entitled to the whole truth. I tried to tell myself that I was a big girl who should have known better. I tried to tell my heart to stop breaking. I tried to force my brain to stop aching. I tried to tell my breathing to become regular again. I didn't know that my thoughts collided with my focus on the road until the car whose lane I had veered on without attention, honked madly after I almost caused a collision. The reality of my life and my heart's misery was as loud as the honk that blared from the other car. I was at a dead-end and I was crucially low on fuel. I was too tired to keep going anywhere.

When I made it home and took my shoes off, my body felt sore. My mind longed for peace as I turned on some music and crawled into bed before allowing my whole body the satisfaction of falling apart. I finally allowed the pain to pour out of me. I gave myself the permission to sob without control. My throat felt as though it was lodged between two walls pressing against it. My skin crawled with discomfort. My eyes bled with tears. Pisces cut me deep and I didn't see it coming. I stared blankly at the ceiling and sobbed over the wounds of my heart.

Laying on my bed, I reminisced about the down-ward spiral I felt in the matters of my heart since Blue. It pained me to acknowledge the lie that I had been living. Pisces didn't love me, and I didn't love him. I justified our chaotic relationship to prove to myself that I was still capable of loving someone even though I no longer recognized who I was. I recalled the times Pisces attacked my sincerity, the times he wanted me to prove my love to him and submit just a little more. I thought about the times he wanted me to see things his way and how he often encouraged me to discard my own discipline and standards to accommodate the kind of love he offered.

When I had little money in my wallet, I gave freely to him whenever he asked. I was generous with everything I had toward Pisces and he knew it. I thought about the eighty-minute round-trip commutes to his house at night and how he never once walked me to the car when I left during midnight. I recalled how he demanded that I text him when I reached home for him to know I was safe. That was the standard I accepted, and not once did I miss the absence of honor in my season with Pisces.

My pillows soaked with tears as the harsh truths unfolded and became clearer. I allowed myself to finally face all that was wrong about my closeness with Pisces from the start. In that year and a half, I learned closely to be molded again as though I was that little girl back in church with the willingness to learn. As I grew closer to Pisces, I learned to be silent and cautious of how much I spoke as not to trigger him. I grew desperate for his love. I wanted to earn it, not knowing all the while that the reason he couldn't give me his heart or the warmth I craved, was because he had already given it to someone else. Then the Spirit reminded me once again, like Blue, Pisces was not God. What I desperately needed and wanted was a touch from God.

PART FIVE

GRACE

CHAPTER 17

Becoming

I WAS WORN OUT FROM heartbreak and bad decisions. I wanted to pray but I felt unequipped to utter a word of prayer. I wanted to be angry, but I couldn't muster the energy to reach anger. I listened to my spirit for the first time in a long time and I heard it whisper a desperate need for peace. I wanted to make peace with everything. I wanted to be at peace with everything, most especially, with myself. I yearned to live in peace. The turmoil I felt within needed the peace of God and after all this time, I no longer wanted to do life my own way.

That weekend, I finally admitted to myself that I was completely lost without God. I felt like a tired wanderer with no place to rest. I needed God and I wanted to be in God's soothing presence again, not just for a moment or a day, but to dwell there. That Sunday, I returned to a place of worship after about six months of hiatus from any place of worship.

I walked into Hempstead Assembly of God with a heavy heart and a desperate need for healing. I was greatly hoping for a word that I still believed could pierce through the heart and convict the soul. I was at a point where I knew if I did not have the word from God to lean on in this place, I would surely die. Then I heard the call.

While in motion, I felt my heart leap with hope as my legs moved toward the front of the church for the altar call. I felt hot tears run down my cheeks as the pastor confirmed through his message that it was indeed time for me to come back home to the house of God. The feeling of release of all I had been carrying since Blue was indescribable. It had been so long since I let myself cry in front of anyone. Yet, here I knelt falling apart in the arms of strangers, wiser older women who held me close in their bosom because they saw my tears and witnessed my weak body tremble at the call of God. That Sunday marked the end of a life I tried to mold without God and the beginning of a life I was trusting God to build from scrap.

At the altar, many memories flashed through my head as I remembered all the places I had been, all the caves I had crawled into seeking protection from the pain that would not go away. I recalled the pain of the bonds unfulfilled between my parents and I, the pain of the bonds of broken friendships that I tried to tie together at all costs, the pain of missed opportunities, the pain of restlessness, the pain of brokenness, the pain of immorality, the pain of loneliness, the pain of my inadequacy to fit in the holes that Grace alone knew were too small to fit what God had planned for me. My tears poured down like a cleansing rain. I had strayed so very far from God, so far from His words. I had strayed so far from safety into the wicked arms of sin and foolishness. But in that moment, I realized that I was not far enough that His grace couldn't reach me. I had not strayed far enough to leave God's sight. He was always watching me, always protecting me, and always waiting on me.

Hempstead Assembly of God became my new church home. In the nine weeks that followed my initial entry into that blessed haven, my feet carried my body without permission to heed the altar call whenever the Spirit spoke to me, which was often. Every word was for me. Every message touched me. Every service gave me something that I was beginning to recognize again as faith. My faith came alive and my spirit longed more for the things of God. I awaited Sunday service to hear that altar call and to run to bow down at the feet of a forgiving God, a kind and merciful God. At His feet, I found forgiveness and mercy like I never thought possible. There, I let the tears wash over me every time. There, I laid my burdens and surrendered my past and pains. It wasn't long before my church life began to take over everything else. I started to feel more sensitive to the temptations that refused to die completely. My growing heart for worship evidently did not yet replace my loneliness and the subtle discomfort since Pisces.

K.L had a quietness about him that drew me in. For about four months of getting to know one another, I fought against the lure to get any closer. I wanted to earn my honor as a woman again. I had to put away my childish and sinful mind of fornication. I wanted to wait. I wanted marriage. I wanted a commitment before God. I needed God's permission to give my body to yet another man and I desired my next to be my last.

I knew not to mistake love for lust, so it was evident to me when my body betrayed me and caved in to the pressure whenever I was close to K.L. His words threatened my resolve when he complemented me on how bold I was as a woman and how much it enticed him. Still, I drew closer. I didn't understand why I was drawn to a man who was adamant about becoming physically intimate with a woman before committing to her. The days and weeks passed by and my steadfastness seemed impermeable until it was not. Again, I stumbled.

It happened abruptly one night after a mutual friend's gathering. I initiated it. The thought worried me but my body still permitted me. I didn't know then that there were spirits outside mine that could lure my mind and body into temptation. I didn't know then that we ought to be more careful about the invites we say yes to. Immediately after my stumble, I sensed the inner turmoil against my new-found peace and freedom. Here I was seeking the guidance of God to walk with Him again, to build me up in faith again, to receive a new anointing again, but in my fleshly living, I created a bed with a man again.

I was convicted by the unsettling feeling that came from the intimacy I shared with K.L. I sensed the difference in feeling condemned and being convicted. I felt more guilty than ashamed because I knew better. There was an unsettling feeling in how God revealed it to me. When I expected to only feel guilty for treating my body with dishonor, this time, I was rebuked by my own spirit for dishonoring K.L. I knowingly served as the temptation that brought him deeper into sin away from God's truth. I served as the fruit that lured K.L. into bed. It hurt deeply to acknowledge that wrong.

In my new knowledge, I was more aware of how broken I really was and how nothing aside the grace of God could make something out of my nothing. It dawned on me that after all this time, if I could still hear the voice of God, if God was still so faithful and merciful to favor me in that way, perhaps I could no longer allow temptation to rule over me. Perhaps I had more God in me than I thought. Perhaps I was not helpless against the luring thoughts of that lustful spirit.

After K.L., I admitted to myself that my reflection in the mirror was still in pieces because the mirror itself was broken. Everything I saw reflected brokenness. How I measured my worth, my growth, my wisdom, my love, my being, was all wrong and out of place. My thoughts were not pure and holy. My heart, though it held good intentions, was still not guarded by God's truth. I was responsible but not disciplined. I was knowledgeable but lacked understanding and wisdom. My deeds weren't evil, but they didn't portray the goodness of God either. Everything was out of place. If I was honest with myself, I had no business flirting with the idea of placing any man anywhere in my life. Nothing and no one else could do but God. I wanted God and God alone to put the pieces back into place. I realized then that if I was going to get where I knew only God could take me, I had to be willing to surrender completely and let God Be God in my life in every way. K.L. had to be my *last temptation*.

These thoughts remained in my mind as the weeks neared for me to graduate college. When the day came for me to stride across the stage as a B.A. degree holder, I praised God for helping me finish. I never deserved it, but God's grace kept me. God's grace kept me from losing my mind and losing my way completely. God's grace blessed me with a family present to embrace me with honor and love. As I posed for pictures with friends and family, I thought to myself how faithful God had always been to me. I took missteps that could have hindered my graduation and the accomplishment I worked hard for, yet, God kept me moving toward it. When my name was called, intently taking one step after the other, I acknowledged all that had transpired in my young adult life between the end of high school and the end of college. I felt as though life and I tussled hard but here I was, winning with my bruises and a limp. I graduated Cum Laude.

The following weeks were filled with deep reflection not on what was next, but on what was. I made many wrong decisions in the past. I was wrong many times about so many things and many people. I knew now that the only thing that had always been right in my life was God even though I repeatedly ignored His presence. As I battled my lingering temptations and sinful reasonings to share my bed with K.L., I realized that I could no longer ignore the company and the need for Christ's lordship in my life again. When it came time for God to make a right out of yet another wrong of mine, God's voice was clear, consistent, and undeniable. I heard a call to move out of my parent's home to the place that God was going to show me. Without question, I moved nearer to the Voice that called me to a new place, a new home, a new realm, and a new being.

CHAPTER 18

Dry Bones

"See, I have taken away your sin, and I will put fine garments on you." (Zechariah 3:4) NIV

"ATLANTA?"

"What are you going to do in Atlanta?"

"Are you moving with your family?"

"You are moving by yourself to Atlanta? For what?"

My friends and family asked the questions out loud, but I dare not admit to them that these were questions I privately asked God. I didn't have a concise answer to give them nor did I have a clear idea to tell myself. All I knew was the consistent, unmistakable call to Atlanta. It was a pull that I couldn't explain outright but it was strong and persistent. I wiggled my responses and kept my answers short. I could not yet share what God was yet to reveal to me. I just knew that I was moving to Atlanta, Georgia.

When I sat down to talk with my parents about my move, I expected a conflict as they too had the same questions as everyone else.

"What is in Atlanta?"

I was surprised by the calmness of my father and mother as I told them that I was going to Atlanta to explore my career options and future. I had not planned my response, so when the words came confidently out of my mouth, it felt as though someone else was in that room with me and guiding my tongue to speak.

Weeks passed and I silently comforted myself at the thought of living so far from Ian, my sister, and even my parents. As much as I welcomed the freedom I was finally going to have in my own space and environment, away from my parents' concerned opinions and occasional intrusions, I dreaded the thought of permanently being away from home. I was anxious as I also said goodbye to the budding friendships from college and work that I had come to appreciate. The feeling of separation began to crawl in about a week before my departure and it took a toll on me. There was the solemn dread of saying goodbye to my precious grandmother, Ajia.

I paid more attention in my time of solitude. I needed to be sure of this life-changing transition. I asked the Spirit many questions. There was silence. I considered pushing back my move on several occassions. I considered working longer and saving more before taking this huge leap. I figured maybe I could take a little more time before I went toward the call to the unknown, but I knew in my spirit that the time was here. I felt strongly that I had to go. I moved to Atlanta, Georgia in August.

In the first three weeks of my arrival at Atlanta, I was uncomfortable. I never knew loneliness could hurt as much as it did. I never knew the anguish from missing a family's love could be so pressing. I cried throughout my first month in Atlanta. I missed Ian badly. I missed Ajia. I wanted to hug Mayus. I wanted to play with Ian. I wanted to feel the closeness of my loved ones. And I missed the anointing of Hempstead Assembly. I didn't start working right away so my days began and ended behind closed doors. There was nowhere to go because I knew no one. I didn't have much of anything to do because I was no longer in school. Most of my days consisted of silence and stillness. I had no idea that my inward journey to newness had already begun. I didn't know that solitude with the One who called me had already been initiated by my obedience to move. I just knew that there was peace in the quiet and assurance in the unfamiliarity of my new surroundings. Then the Voice spoke again, and the messages poured.

I heard as a young girl that the first cut was the deepest. Blue was my first and deepest cut. The years that passed may have provided many layers of temporary covering but moving to Atlanta and being stirred up by the past, was prove that the injury Blue caused to my heart was yet to be healed. I recall a time when my thoughts toward Blue was nothing short of hate. I despised the thought of him and the bitter history we shared. I hoped he would suffer terribly like I did when he betrayed me and left my vulnerability open for a stranger to see. It is one thing to be harmed by the ones who claim to love you, but it is a different kind of battle when the ones who claim to love you, lend others the weapons to use against you. Blue did that to me. I had grown accustomed to the voices in the world around me that told me that I was entitled to the anger and disharmony I held on to by not forgiving but forgetting Blue. It was okay to never speak of him or to him again. Time, they say, heals all wounds. That should do it, they said. Over the years, I embraced the creed the idea that I would get over it because time would eventually heal. I listened earnestly to many who told me that I just needed to learn to love another, move on, leave the past alone, grow up, and let it all go.

Before I left New York, I tried to make peace with everything and everyone I was leaving there. During my time at Hempstead Assembly, one of my most prevalent prayers to God was to be granted the heart to forgive others as God had forgiven me. I wanted to forgive everything that I deemed an offense in my past. I wanted to get out of the trap of offense. I needed to be free of the strongholds of an un-forgiving heart. Wanting to forgive is not the same as knowing how to forgive. Forgiveness can only happen with the grace of God. I am convinced that it is the Spirit of God that enables us to truly forgive others who have hurt us. On my road to forgiving, I started with the first one that mattered the most, Blue. It was a long, tiring, and overwhelming path to cross but there was no bridge over it or any other way around it. I had to go through it. I heard God's orders loud and clear. I was compelled to reach out to Blue through my contact with his brother and to open my heart for the restoration that God was about to do in a way that was much bigger than me.

As expected, I was initially met with resistance and unease as old wounds were re-opened. It was an uncomfortable place that I was told would soon yield the comfort I never knew I needed. During my last few days in New York, Blue and I saw each other again. I was astonished by the sentiments that sprung up. Although we had both grown and matured in the passing years since our separation, the air of familiarity shined brightly during our conversation. We argued, yelled, and disagreed on truths and lies. I cried a lot. But God had His way. As we both dug up the lies, we had long buried when we went our separate ways five years prior, God's truth unfolded and freed the skeletons in both of our closets. Some of those dry bones rode with me to Atlanta.

In Atlanta, God graced me to only heard the Voice of truth. Harmony was the first of many miracles that God granted me in Atlanta. God's spirit told me to believe in the hope of harmony and the power of forgiveness. So, I did. The miracle of forgiveness that unfolded before me tore me apart in the most amazing way as it broke through the walls of falsehoods, I had guarded myself with after Blue. I saw God work. I felt chains loosen when Blue asked for my forgiveness and apologized for not only betraying our friendship, but also for abusing the love I felt for him. I felt myself loosen my own grip on un-forgiveness. My heart begged to be free. My spirit longed to finally release the heartache I had held on to inadvertently through the years. This was my first miracle. This was true forgiveness, and this was God.

There were no long overdue professions of love lost or intentions of rekindling any fires. There was only harmony. Somehow, someway, outside our doing, harmony was restored between Blue and I and we miraculously began to talk as friends again. In due time, the abuses, insults, and blames that we initially came with passed away in our conversations. There was only peace and harmony. I then began to learn that harmony was a place of God. This place of harmony spilled over on the other areas of my life as I sought God in a new way in this new place. This was overflow. I felt driven by peace, wanting to right the wrongs I made. I braced myself for another miracle of harmony as I myself sought forgiveness and understanding from a person that I parted ways with in amicably.

I had a near-physical altercation with a young lady during my last year in college. It was earlier in the year. The situation had bubbled up for about a year with the surrounding forces of gossip and malicious communication. When the anger erupted, I almost came to blows with her. For about ten minutes, we both hurled insults and profanity at one another as other people in our student-run radio organization witnessed it in disbelief. I too was in disbelief about how angry I got and how close I came to engage in a physical confrontation on campus. I imagined the consequences that would have followed. A possible arrest or an expulsion could have been the result. I thank God for the intervention of grace and the self-control to not completely lose my head. I ultimately walked away before things got out of control but the silent displeasure that I felt toward this person remained. Whether it was my stubbornness, ignorance, or uncertainty then, I couldn't bring myself to reach out to her while I was still in New York. I had imagined the many ways she could respond so I willed myself out of the responsibility of taking the first step towards forgiveness.

In Atlanta, when the displeasure sipped back to the surface during my time of renewal and restoration, I knew I had to go and break the yoke of malice that the enemy tied between myself and this person. If God could restore goodness between Blue and I, surely there was room for more miracles. My feelings were different because the power of God's harmony told me different. It told me to adhere to the Spirit and to seek out this individual, to admit my wrongs so the enemy didn't have room to exploit the sore place. So, I reached out to her and prepared myself for a possible dismissal or refusal to accept my peace offering.

As God would have it, she responded the very same day I reached out to her. Not only did she commend me for reaching out first after all the time that had passed, she thanked me too. She told me how remorseful she was for the role she also played in the events that led to our heated verbal confrontation. I was amazed. The ease of our interaction was unexpected and comforting.

Furthermore, she shared her own testimony of how God had done something remarkable in her, changing her life for the better. She expressed how grateful she was to be on a journey that allowed room for forgiveness and harmony. More awe struck me because I knew this was God. I think I read her response message at least five times over to believe that it was truly happening. I realized after that God had indeed gone before me, turning her heart warm, to make way for the harmony that was to follow. I wonder if harmony would have ever been restored between us if I never reached out. I wonder if we both would have received the blessing of forgiving and being forgiven if we never opened our hearts to the possibility of God's harmony in the first place. I held on to this moment. In a significant yet subtle way, God showed me His power and presence. But it was only the beginning.

I moved to Atlanta with half of the savings goal I originally intended. I was anxious at the thought of lack and needing more when I arrived in Atlanta. My job was not yet secure and I was no longer in school so there were no student opportunities that promised a source of income. Truly, I was petrified. I had an apartment that needed furniture. An empty refrigerator needed to be filled with groceries. A working stove needed to be used with pots. But no need was greater than the need to get around. About a thousand dollars of the five thousand I had, went into car rental in the first three weeks of my move. There was the cost for a van to drive down to Atlanta. Then the cost of renting a smaller car in my name after I arrived. Being under the age of twenty-five also cost me a little more than just renting the car. Two weeks came and went, and I had to return the car to the car rental. Then there came the cost of the transportation back home without a car. It quickly dawned on me that I needed a car and I needed one fast.

The thought of the inevitable overwhelmed me. I would have to finance a car and everything would have to go under my name. At twenty-three, I was troubled by the emerging responsibility of adulthood. I didn't know where to begin or how to even negotiate buying a car. The former cars I owned were pre-owned and purchased through my brother's careful and knowledgeable judgment. My brother took care of those details in the past, but the time had come for me to handle it on my own.

My credit was good but very short in history – less than two years short. I didn't know what car or make would serve me best. And the most pressing matter of course, I had no money to put down on a car. I went anyway to the Hertz car dealership that my brother recommended. On my third visit there, I found a car that was reasonably priced, and I prayed to God to take care of the rest. Hopeful and anxious, I filled in the paperwork and listened attentively to the salesperson as he gently went over my options. The salesman said that it would be nearly impossible to get the car without at least a thousand dollar down-payment.

I sat still and the panic in my eyes was more evident. I stared blankly at the unopened bottle of water that was offered to me. My worry quenched my thirst. I explained for the third time to the salesman that I didn't have that much money to put down, but I could come up with half. I saw the empathy and powerlessness in his expression. And when he left the office for the fourth time, I inwardly began to call on God louder. Almost two hours had passed waiting. Then the phone calls to the lenders began. I stepped outside to make a panic call to my brother, who had also recently moved to another state a few months before I moved to Atlanta. Surely Mike had his own financial obligations and it pained me to make the call, but I really needed the car and I needed to make sure I knocked on every door available to me before accepting that it was not meant to be.

By the end of the call, Mike gave me the possibility of loaning me the money should it come down to it. I was grateful. When the salesman called me back into the office to sit down with the finance manager, I sunk slowly into the seat and waited for what looked like an expected defeat. I raised my head and was met with the warmth and sincerity of an older gentleman.

Eight banks. The finance manager called eight different banks and wouldn't stop until I was approved for the loan. Grace. Then he informed me that I didn't need to put any money down. Abundant grace. And he sealed the message of hope by telling me that my first payment was not due for another five weeks. Abundant, merciful, unexplainable grace. This. Was. God. With no job, or even a pending interview, with a new credit history, with all the odds against the outcome I needed, God graced me with a car. I had a car, an apartment, and all the bills that came with it all under my name and I was unemployed. Grace did that. God did that. This was yet another miracle. I looked for more.

Weeks turned to months and I sensed the shift inside me. I felt dry bones come to life as I began to seek God in this secret place where God, His spirit, and I met and conversed as One. I wanted more of God. I wanted to see Him work. It was not enough to know He was always working, I wanted to see the work, to be plugged into the work. I yearned to be aligned with the Most-High and to walk with Him as He walked through my life. It was time for me to find a church home.

I was hesitant. A part of me was tired of church and its regulations. A small part of me was tired of church folk who judged and discounted everyone else that didn't live the church-prescribed lifestyle. Despite my worries, the bigger part of me that felt it necessary to feed my spirit, pushed me to seek a church home. If there was anything to note about Atlanta, much like the rest of Georgia and the South in general, there were tons of churches all around. It felt like there was one on every corner, at every exit, and by the turn of every other traffic light. There were many churches to choose from, but it was not to be my choice. I needed to find the one that God chose. September had just begun.

The first church I walked into was neighbored to the left of my apartment complex. It was a Lutheran fold. They welcomed me with open arms and sincere smiles. But I didn't feel the inward touch to settle.

The following week, I walked into a non-denominational church that was neighbored to the right of my new home in Atlanta. We took communion, the service was good, but still, no touch. I was waiting for something to click in place. I was waiting for that inward confirmation from God, that inward peace that will assure me of my footing and placement to be nurtured spiritually again. Two churches down and I really started to feel like a sojourner with no place to lay her head and heart for worship and nurture. At the end of the week, I spotted another church a few minutes' drive down the block from my place. It was the same road as my apartment home, but it stretched and cut through other parts of the neighborhood. The church was situated quietly and noticeably on a slight hill at a nearby intersection. I drove past it several times before, looked at the structure, but never quite saw the church. But it was right there all along. That Friday, I saw it.

The following Sunday when I walked into Mt. Zion Baptist Church, I was greeted by the sweetest melody. I felt something powerful breathe on me but it was not until the altar call, that I realized what that immediate embrace was. It felt like I was walking into the loving arms of my Father. I walked slowly to the stairs of the altar and knelt obediently. There, I felt the touch. Literally, I felt a warm hand touch my shoulder, then my hand, and a sweet older lady asked, "Is it okay if I pray with you?" The tears welled up, then they fell quietly. I nodded in agreement. I heard the voice of the Lord say, "Here. I AM here and this is where I want you." I felt like Mt. Zion Baptist church had been set apart and waiting for me to come in. I found my new church home.

Three Sundays later, I was baptized. It was October.

CHAPTER 19

A High Calling

EVERYTHING I THOUGHT I KNEW, I did not. I heard it preach too often as a child and I thought I knew what it meant to know God and to love Him with all my heart, mind, and soul. I thought I was good and upright because of my intentions to be good and upright but that moment of destiny that called my body into the clear waters, changed all I thought I knew. Death was lurking again and a new birth was waiting its turn.

Wise ones say that it takes a village to raise a child. My maternal grandmother, Alhaja (Al-Haa-Ja) was the head of my village. Back in Nigeria, a woman of the Muslim faith was referred to as Alhaja, and a man, Alhaji. We called her Ajia for short. A devout woman, Ajia was a worshipper whose prayers for her family never wavered.

In Nigeria, Ajia was the most constant source of love and stability in my life because she was always present. There were times where it was just me and her in the house. She would pray and I would find something to do for play. She was the only Muslim I had a chance to know intimately. She would teach us sayings in Islam as she prayed it. She did not attend school but Ajia's wisdom was divine. She was a special woman, one who was especially generous. Ajia gave what she had without hesitation. Her kindness never faltered toward anyone.

When she cooked, everyone, including her landlord's children, shared in the meal. Ajia literally fed and raised generations. She was the matriarch on my mother's side of the family, but her influence extended to my father's side as well. She was strong, solid, and unwavering in her love. We often forgot that she was in her 70s. As a young child, I was oblivious to her age because all I saw when I looked at Ajia, was strength and movement. She was always on the move. She was usually on her way to or from the Mosque, cooking lunch, cooking dinner, cooking with our landlady, or helping to take care of another new- born. Ajia was a pillar for her family and community. She was as gentle and loving, as she was stern and influential. Her presence was always felt even when she was silent. Her power and shield coursed through the entire house whether she was there or not.

Her house was no big space, but it served as a haven in my childhood. It was a living room, one room with a bed in it, a hallway that led to the kitchen, a bathroom, and a separate toilet. Ajia's place was the home that every member of the family knew. Throughout my childhood in Nigeria, her living room floor was my oldest bedrest. No beds or pillows needed, just mats and whatever covering was available.

Armed robbery was prevalent in Lagos, Nigeria. I often heard about it happening or saw it in a movie but was not prepared for it to happen to me and my family.

That night, we were in Ajia's living room waiting for dinner to be finished. We were ten in all, talking and laughing, until Ajia and two neighbors walked in with three big men following closely behind them. The big rifles they carried also trailed closely behind Ajia and the others. Each of the men also had another weapon in hand. The space in the room got smaller as they entered. Fear and uncertainty filled the space. Within seconds, the men sternly commanded everyone to kneel with our faces to the ground. They need not say it more than once. My three-year-old cousin was the youngest person in the room. When one of the armed robbers grabbed him and tossed him in the hands of my older cousin, I feared the worst. The armed man then demanded that the toddler be kept especially quiet throughout their operation.

It was like a bad movie, and I was not certain it would be a good ending for all of us. Most of the movies I had ever seen with robberies always ended with death, kidnapping, or rape.

With all our faces to the ground, Ajia begged us all in her calming voice to listen to the armed men and to do as we were instructed. I will never forget how she kindly asked one of the men to turn off the stove to halt the dinner preparation they interrupted so as not to cause a fire. Surprisingly, he complied. Unlike most of us, Ajia was not frantic, nor did she show any fear. I watched closely as Ajia wore her peace with resolve and I know that alone gave courage to the rest of us to follow her lead.

With heads still bowed to the ground in compliance, we all did the only thing we could do in the helpless situation that was before us. We prayed. Some of us prayed quietly with words, while the rest of us prayed with our tears. We all hoped to live another day and tell the story. That was sixteen years ago. Grace made sure that everyone lived through the terrifying ordeal. No one was injured physically but the trauma of that night was a lasting one for many years. I learned very young that God always protects His own no matter how dark the night, or how powerful the enemy appears to be.

On the day of her husband's burial, Ajia extended the same comfort to us all as she did the night of the robbery. All the kids cried as the Muslim community prepared to carry my grandpa's body to the burial site. After the preparation, his body was wrapped in new mats to be carried away, as was the sacred Islam tradition. Even in her own loss and pain, Ajia assumed a comforting role for the rest of her family. She called and gathered us all in the living room to shield us from the walk of grandpa's body. She called us with love and strength and tried to ease our heartbreak as best as she could. I remember how she held back her own tears to wipe ours away in compassion. That was Ajia – kind, warm, and strong.

So, the day Mayus, Mike, and I boarded the plane to America in December 2001, saying goodbye to Ajia was harder than saying goodbye to my own mother because I did not know if or when next I would see her again. I considered how greatly I would miss her sweet cooking and sweeter love, and my heart broke at how far distance would separate us for as long as it was about to.

Thirteen years long.

I lived without the Ajia's warm embrace and kisses, without the sweet sound of her prayers, for thirteen years. In that time, I was uncertain about seeing Ajia again before her time on earth was done. I had started to cherish the sound of her voice over the phone more often, seeing as it was my only form of contact and connection to her. I was grateful to at least speak to her. Before Ma came over to America, Ajia was always by her side whenever my father made a call to Nigeria or when my mother called us in America. Time made no promises and although it felt naïve of me, I harbored great hope to see Ajia again before she left this world. That desperate hope became fruitful in late 2013 when my father informed us that Ajia was coming to America for a short while. I danced in joyous disbelief.

Two weeks after my father's announcement, the joy in my heart poured out through my tears as I knelt in greeting before Ajia as a twenty-two- year-old. As expected, it took her a moment to recognize who I was, not because her sight was failing, but because I was evidently not the little girl that clung tight to her body-wrap thirteen years back. I was overwhelmed with emotions as I remembered all she meant to me. I will forever treasure the moment she realized who knelt before her weeping. She hugged me tightly and hailed my name in our native dialect as she used to back home. It was a blessed reunion.

Living with Ajia again was a blessing that kept on giving. I never realized how influential her presence in my adult life was until I commenced the journey of writing this book. Her grace and generosity had not changed. I even saved the few single dollars she gave me as a gift. I placed them in a safe box, refusing to spend the money. It was merely four dollars in the naked eye but was worth more than gold in my heart because Ajia gave it to me.

In my last year of college, Ajia would stay up for my sake in her room, refusing to sleep until I got home. She would often save a piece of meat from her dinner to give to me when I came to greet her good night. Her smile always radiated the room and gave my day a goodness I could not explain. It was something about the gentleness in her eyes and the softness of her voice that simply overtook me every single time I made my way into her room. Her love was soothing with just one look. What a blessing it was to have such a kind spirit as a grandmother. She was my queen. I even looked forward to braiding her soft gray hair from time to time and especially how she would pray over me as her form of gratitude. Ajia's love was endless.

When God called me to Atlanta, I feared the inevitable. As my preparation to relocate began, the melancholy sentiments stirred up from the pits of my belly that this goodbye to Ajia was the final one. I knew that something was preparing me for Ajia's own departure the very last time I braided her hair before I left for Atlanta. Something in me couldn't let go of the ball of hair that the comb pulled from her graceful head. I stared intently at the gray hairball in my hand before sliding it into my pocket. I couldn't throw it away this time. It was mine to keep.

I'm amazed by how the spirit of God gives peace even before a storm hits. I'm grateful for the comfort in God that settled within me before tragedy come knocking. All too often, we fail to acknowledge the power and presence of God in us as He fulfills His word to keep us and be our comforter even when we do not see the discomfort ahead. I had only been settled in Atlanta for about six weeks before the yearning for Ajia began. I knew I missed her greatly like I missed the rest of the family, but this was different. I felt her calling me. I felt her pulling me to come home and see her. I felt unsettled in the nights leading to my first visit back to New York. Something kept telling me gently but urgently that I had to go see Ajia. I had just been hired at my new job when I asked my manager for a grace period before starting. I had to go to New York. I had to see Ajia.

A few days later, I arrived in New York, eager to see my family. About fifteen minutes after my plane landed at LaGuardia airport, I had just retrieved my luggage when Mayus called me. She sounded hesitant, speaking slowly but intent. Mayus informed me that Ajia was admitted to the hospital two weeks prior and was currently in the ICU. The shock came before the anger. I was shocked that my entire family, including my mother and father whom I had spoken to daily since my move to Atlanta, purposely hid the news from me. It was during that call with Mayus that I thought back to the evasiveness of my parents whenever I asked about Ajia on the phone. They would tell me that she was sleeping and of course I never asked them to wake her. They lied to me. I was hurt that they didn't tell me of Ajia's condition. I would've come home sooner. I was angry that they kept me away from home, away from Ajia, knowing that she could be called by the Lord at any moment. I scolded Mayus in between my sobs until I remembered the peace that was settling inside me for the past three weeks. My shock subsided.

I was overwhelmed with vulnerability as my week-long visit to New York neared its end. I was not ready to say goodbye. I was not ready to never see my Ajia again. There was so much I wanted to do to take care of her. I wished for my children to see her and feel the warmth and wisdom that radiated from her presence alone. I was not ready to let go of the first woman I ever knew and loved. I prayed fervently every day. I was aware of nature taking its course, and even more aware that God was preparing us to release Ajia to Him. I knew that God was getting ready to take back what He gave so I begged God to give us just a little more time. I also begged God to consider giving even more time than I was praying for. But I left New York in surrender to the will of God and the strength we would all need to let Ajia go when the time came. God hearkened to all our desperate cries and pleas in that time.

The same week I returned to Atlanta, Ajia left the ICU and got to travel back home to Nigeria about a week and a half later. That was a prayer answered all by itself. We had all feared that she wouldn't make it back to be with the rest of the family before she passed. We dreaded having to send news that Ajia would not be coming back alive. Between the time that Ajia was first admitted into the hospital here in the States, and the time of her passing, my family grew stronger and closer than we had ever been. We all knew that the loss ahead would take its toll on each of us and we would need each other's strength and support along with God's grace to remain grounded in love and faith through it.

Ajia went to be with the Lord about a month after she arrived back home in Nigeria. She was ninety years old. When my brother who was residing in California delivered the news to me via Skype, I finally made way for the heartache that has been knocking quietly for weeks. My heart broke calmly as I welcomed the greatest loss I had ever experienced through death. My Ajia was gone and my heart was broken. I missed her already the moment Mike told me.

Losing Ajia taught me that true love soars even the sight of death. I cherished Ajia. I cherished her place in my life from birth as one who held me, fed me, taught me, played with me, and never stopped praying for me. I close my eyes from time to time to relish in the vision of her walking with grace into the gates of heaven. I imagine how joyous the heavenly hosts were to welcome her back Home. I miss her greatly every now and then, but I thank God for the gift of love and deep wisdom that she was and will forever be to the many lives she raised and nurtured. To her, I solemnly sing,

My Sweet Ajia,
A warrior that never fell,
Grace held you up,
Truth kept you firm,
You were the epitome of strength,
An anchor of peace and harmony,
Your heart was a castle of love and warmth,
So many memories flood in,
But the lasting feeling for all,
Is love. You were love.
Everything you did was with love.
Everything you said was with love.
You raised generations with love.
I watched you brew boys into men with love.
I watched you teach girls to become good women with
love.

I was thankfully one of them.
I am so honored to be one of whom you touched,
literally and figuratively.
My heart breaks at the thought of never again holding
you,
Or braiding your beautiful gray hair,
Or simply laying my head on your sweet bosom,
But at the same time, my soul leaps with joy for the
celebration here on earth and in heaven,
May paradise kiss your golden heart with the peace and
great welcome it deserves.
Thank you for your unending presence.
Thank you for being the blessing that God called you to
be in my life.
My love for you soars even as I write,
Even as my tears fall at your departure,
Even as my heart breaks for longing to behold your
loving eyes again,
I love you so dearly,
You mean so much to me,
You will live forever in my heart.
I cling to the lasting peace and warmth of
your kind spirit,
I pray you sleep and live well in paradise.
Goodnight my sweet, loving, beautiful queen.

CHAPTER 20

But Grace

THE SECOND TO MY LAST semester in college threatened to be my last when I lost my USB drive. My entire academic career and most of my life's memories in film and picture was saved on that one device. College and scholarship essays dating back to high school, pictures and memories I wouldn't trade for anything, and a significant amount of my life accomplishments were saved on the USB. It validated more than I wished to admit. Then I lost it. I can't explain how or when I misplaced it. I just know that I had it when that week began, and it was nowhere to be found when that horrible week ended.

I looked everywhere. I searched every room I ever ventured into all over campus. At home, I tore my room upside down trying to find it. I went back and forth to the lost and found office to no avail. It was an exhausting and emotional search that yielded no finding. I was too devastated to cry. But losing my USB paused me. I strongly considered dropping out of school that May. I was angry at myself for being irresponsible and absent-minded. I was madder that this little device was my proof of the life I have worked hard to build through academia. When it was no more, I felt like I had nothing to show for my life experiences. My USB drive was my badge of adequacy and just like that, without warning, it disappeared.

This experience mirrored exactly how I felt when the shedding of my former self began. Everything I ever thought I needed to validate who I was and what I was worth had to become lost in the cleansing of my spirit. This time, it was I who had to surrender willingly to the loss of everything to be something for God.

After Ajia's death, I clung to God for more than comfort. Since I was now in my own place in Atlanta, I grieved alone. My family tried to extend their comfort as best as they could, but I was still alone. Some nights, I felt the ache in my chest about Ajia's departure. It crushed me each time and I permitted my sorrow to flow freely through my tears. Even in this place of grief, I felt God's arms around me, assuring me that this too was meant for my rebirth. I needed to rely solely on the comfort and strength of God in my anguish. I especially needed the presence of God to stay still as I began to fill the changes in me.

In my time of grief, my spiritual appetite took over and I longed to feed this newness on the inside. I was like a baby, a newborn child, suckling on the word of God, eager to learn the ways of my Father, excited to crawl, then walk before my Father in faith and to follow wherever He led me. I had to learn to deeply trust God again and to grow into the being that my Father intended. All I wanted was intimacy with God. There were no more gray areas. I just wanted to be with God, bask in His presence, hear His word, and be in the peace that only God gave. I felt my spirit begin to recoil to the exposure of things or people that did not align with my desire to always be with God and in God.

As my dearest Ajia was called to the clouds, I too felt the calling to higher realms. Another death was taking place inside of me. A change, a cleanse, a purification, a loud and quiet process of molding and polishing was taking place on the inside. Some things had to be cut, ripped, smashed to pieces, scratched away, washed away, and pulled apart for God to work. My attitudes, habits, beliefs, ideologies, behaviors, and mannerisms all had to be remolded by the Potter. There was peace as there was discomfort. There was joy as there was sorrow. There was celebration as there was mourning. Life and death grew on the inside. Slowly but surely, the me I used to be, began to fall under the pressure and determination of my becoming.

Lower went my pride and selfishness, and higher became my need for patience and humility. I was not the same. My thoughts were not the same. My speech was not the same. My sight was not the same. I was born-again. I was renewed. A garment of righteousness was being fitted on me by my Father and I stood obediently in amazement at the mercy of Him who never stopped loving me. I gradually fell to my knees as I was weakened daily by the weight of my past wrongs and stumbles. Day by day, revelations about where I had been and why, poured into my spirit as I grew in obedience and worship. My time with God became my way of life. It was a necessity to wake up in stillness to hear my Father, sit with Him, talk with Him, and bask in His presence. I started to live life with God and for God.

The music I listened to, the TV shows I watched, the books I read, and the people I kept company with, all had to come in alignment with the new life that was me. The substance I allowed into my mind and spirit either fed it or malnourished it. It had to be one or the other. And when the birth in me began to burst forth through me, my person changed too. I couldn't claim to honor the mark of God on me and still wear revealing attire that didn't reflect or cover that honor. I couldn't profess the love of God and speak life then with the same tongue, curse or speak vulgar utterances that dishonored my mouth of praise. I was changing.

I was starting to experience the saying I heard as a child of what it felt like to be born-again and washed by the blood of Christ. Eagerly, I walked closer to the secret place. Much was revealed to me about myself, about those around me, and about Whose I was. My spirit soon began to crush my idea of friendship and friendliness. I was in awe because I knew that grace walked closer to me and with me. I was learning who God was and what it meant to be created in God's image.

At church, I embraced the love of an amazing fold whose love for Christ was evident in their love for each other. I eagerly awaited every church event for a chance to be among God's people and be surrounded by a kind of love I had never known before. This was the Body of Christ and I belonged in it. I volunteered to help in any and every way I could. I jumped at the chance to be present at our church community events, witnessing fathers and husbands honor their wives and families and set the example for the younger men to follow. I sat back and observed the leadership God ordained in each person in their various roles. They were leaders by the power of God and it amazed me to be a witness of it all. This was grace.

Grace positioned me to witness many lost children of God, young and old, surrender to the power of His presence and touch each Sunday. Grace sat me in a place of wonder. More and more, I succumbed to the call to become what God alone wanted me to be. I needed the word of God now more than ever and I sought it fervently in every way possible. Aside from the strong desire to really absorb the word of God in the Bible, I dived into sermons on YouTube. I opened my ears and heart to receive the word however God sent it my way on a given day. I even became consistent in the listening of gospel or contemporary Christian music stations on my radio. Whatever stirred my spirit and desire for the will of God was what my attention was given to. Nothing else sufficed.

In November of that year, a sermon gripped me. It was a word pertaining to my sacred relationship to God as a woman of God and a re-dedication to Christ as His bride. That word poured into me the wisdom and true essence of my purity in Christ. As I fed my spirit, it too fed me. Among the many truths that mercy and grace granted me, this was one of the most powerful. Gone were the days that perversion had its way with my mind or body. I felt a divine possession erupt from within as I heard the words that reminded me of the price Christ paid to save me, and to have me for His own. I was the bride of the living Christ. There was a pain and praise held in the release of the guilt I had clung to for many years. The Lord still loved me and still wanted me no matter what I had done. God refused to leave me in my filth. It was the mercy of God and the grace through Christ that picked me up along the way when HE saw me laying in the filth of sin and sexual immorality. After all I had done, after all I had said, after all I felt I wasted, what was left of me, was still good enough for Christ to claim as His. This was amazing grace.

It is a wonderful thing indeed to be transformed when your mind is healed from the abuse of sin. It was a place of awe to receive the crown that my Father adorned me with before and even after all I had done. Meditating daily on the words of the sermon, I began to look in the mirror more and saw differently. I no longer saw the images of filth, damage, or uncleanliness. The reflection of God began to stare back at me as I received the full glory of Christ in my everyday living. I knew it was not my doing. It was the Holy Spirit of God renewing my mind, guiding me, directing me, and leading me closer to the light of God that was in me. The Spirit of God brought to life the significance of Calvary. I walked closer to the cross. I now finally understood that Christ died so I could live like this. It was His death that gave me the perfection and righteousness that this world could never give nor take away from me. I finally believed it.

I finally believed that I was worthy because He called me worthy. I finally believed that I was worth dying for because He did go to the cross for me. This was amazing saving grace!

Before everyone else could see the change on me, I sought the spiritual sight of God to see God right in all things. I prayed without ceasing to not just see things but to see through them. God answered. The word of God became prevalent in my daily thought and speech. The challenges of living in a new place with no friends or family did not evade me. Times got lonely. I cooked alone. I ate alone. I prayed alone. I danced alone. I watched TV alone. I read alone. But I never walked alone. The Spirit of God reminded me that I only felt alone but I was never alone. The Spirit of God was with me. I could not hug or touch it, but I know It could hug and touch me and it had to be enough for the season of solitude that God wanted for me.

Financially, a sense of stability in Atlanta took root. November came and disrupted that growing stability. My manager and I shared a love for God. Three and a half weeks after I started working, my manager's promotion separated us. He was promoted to New York, to the very same store I left when I moved to Atlanta. He revealed to me during the initial interview that this very store was the one he also left four years prior when he moved to Atlanta. We both worked under the same manager in different times. I was amazed at the intentionality of God. It dawned on me then, that absolutely nothing is co-incidental. God is always in control. Everything falls into motion according to His All-knowing plans.

By December, my manager had devised a short-term plan that would assist my upward movement on the company ladder. I intended to work in New York and go back and forth to Atlanta in a three-month period to see what it would yield. I would be working under my manager's guidance and learning all that I needed to know at an even faster pace to get to the next phase of leadership within the company. It seemed practical since I had been with the company now for a little over a year. Thoughts of graduate school and its costs loomed as I too began to embrace the idea of earning more to save up for my near future. Nevertheless, I felt the resolve to let God decide and for His will to be done.

It turned out that God had other plans. I was again reminded of His intentionality and absolute control at the end of December when the Spirit rejected my will to move up the company ladder. God reminded me of His will and purpose for bringing me to Atlanta and it was not to move up on the ladder in a retail company, no matter how prosperous it seemed. Furthermore, to my dismay, God revealed to me that this job was not part of the divine plan for my future.

The clarity of God's voice was unmistakable when I heard it again a few days before Christmas. The holiday craze was not yet over and the long and demanding hours at work were painful. It had been a week since I heard God's refusal about me going back to New York for the sake of my job.

"January fifteenth," said the Voice.

"What about January fifteenth?" Silence.

The third of January was my sister's birthday, and the sixteenth was my brother-in-law's birthday, so I knew I was not missing a birthday. I had no events planned. There was nothing significant going on at church on January fifteenth. So, what was January fifteenth?

"Leave your job on January fifteenth."

I was getting along well with my co-workers. My new manager appreciated my strong work ethic. I was favored in getting a stream of good clientele. Arduous as it was to drive seventy miles each day, I was grateful to have a job. But I knew the voice of God when I heard it and it was clear enough. No job meant no money to pay the bills. Rent bill, insurance bill, car loan bill, credit card bill, and grocery bill.

"Lord can you please clarify?" I inwardly asked.

Again, as calmly as the first time, I heard, "Leave your job on January 15th. It is time to tell others about Me." I was shaken by God's word to me, but. I knew that obedience was all I had to give, and He would do the rest.

I thought sharing my testimony with the people I met in Atlanta and the old friends I knew in New York was enough. I thought my testimony was common and I did not need to say more but I was wrong. The works that God has done in my life, through my life cannot all be contained in these words. I didn't know that God was getting me ready to write about this journey of unfailing grace.

I was filled with angst in the next few days as I shared the revelation with my family during their Christmas visit. As expected, the question poured out once again as it did back when I heard God's call to move, and as it was back then, I had little to no response aside from my open willingness to obey what God told me. They all left and my distressed yet determined spirit was my focus again. I had an order to obey before the new year came. I gave in my two-week notice on December 30th and prayed desperately for the discernment to not miss what God was about to do.

During our conversation, my new manager, bewildered by my abrupt notice, informed me that the management trainee program was to take place late January and he had submitted my name as his strongest prospect. I laughed at the humor of God. I had the exact same conversation with my former manager back in New York a couple of weeks prior to my leave for Atlanta. This second time around, I saw God smile. He was intentional about His plan for me. He was ordering my steps, this time, away from Nordstrom.

As terrified as I was of the near future, I could not deny the audacious spirit that had become my new shadow. I was confident in the Spirit of God in me and nothing else. I wondered what would come next and how I could navigate this journey in a new state all by myself without a job again. Every time the thoughts of doubts and uncertainty flooded my soul, I heard God say, "I AM. Trust Me." The year ended with flashes of possibilities marking my mind as I considered the limitless power of God.

On the first day of the new year, I felt that power move my hands to begin the work to water the seed of purpose and promise. Mygraceuntold.com became a reality. After many months of complacency, I created my blogsite under my name with my own money. I thank God for Mike who walked me through the process of registering my site. Then the messages steadily poured in my spirit. Before a new sun rose, I had a word from God not only to share with others, but to share with myself. My journey became a rooted substance in what I was sharing with others.

I began to watch for God closely each new day, to see what He was trying to show me even in the subtlest way. The Holy Spirit indeed became my dominant companion. We sat together, sometimes in silence. We listened to praise songs together. We watched sermons together. We worshiped together. We talked with one another. It was the greatest height of intimacy I had ever felt in my entire life. This was Grace. This was Love. This was Honor. This was Truth. And it was mine. As my blogposts piled up, the buried parts of my past rose again. This time, torment did not come with remembering, rather, the memories of my brokenness spilled onto these pages that you are now reading. God was birthing this book. I thought I was only to tell a story. But I soon realized that I am the story and I was part of God's story of amazing grace.

I still wonder sometimes how a wretch like me was granted such beauty for my ashes. I still think deeply at times how God's mercy found me and tore me away from despair when it was me who spit in the face of Love in the first place. I had always believed in God, but I stopped following Him. The moment I gave what I believed to be my only honor to Blue, was the same instant I stopped following all of God's instructions as a Father and a friend. I validated breaking one of God's word and it catapulted me into a world of disobedience. Funny how you can be a believer in God but be farthest from Him because you think your waywardness is masked by your belief. Losing my virginity pushed me into a dangerous un-ending field of loss and regret, which then thrust me into a world of immorality and defiance. I realize that I got by because I was more discreet than others about the brokenness that was my sinking sand. But Grace kept me.

I remember the moments so vividly. I remember the moment when innocence was lost, the moment purity was stained, the moment my love became depraved, the moment truth was discarded, the moment sin was embraced, the moment evil made its way in, the moment I shed the seed that was the result of a perverted love, the moment a burial took place on the inside, the moment a mask was created, the moment pain became home, the moment anger became a friend, the moment the road widened, the moment foolishness took the reins, the moment my strength collapsed, the moment freewill caged me, the moment the grave was dug, the moment I stumbled and violently fell never to rise again, I remember the moment I gave up all hope, the moment faith no longer lived in me, and the moment I closed my eyes. Then came the moment I woke up in the arms of God's grace.

Every fleeting moment came after I ran away from the Love that always ran with me, Love that promised to never leave nor forsake me. God saw how far I would run even before I took my first steps and yet He went before me to position grace ahead of time. Those fleeting moments spanned the last seven years and deposited me here, to this place of awe and gratitude, that a Love so unconditional truly existed, a Love that I could never earn nor deserve. Every heartbreak, every disappointment, every cut, wound, and scar, was a journey on its own that guided me from realm to realm so I would come to see the fullness and beauty of that unconditional Love that saved my life when it gave up His life on that sacred hill at Calvary.

After Blue, chaos and disharmony chased relentlessly after me. I could never get too far away from the place where guilt and shame had me shackled. The chains clung to my feet and I carried them in acceptance as a part of my portion. When weariness took over, I laid there and covered myself with the blanket of deception and filth. Truth is, I expected to die there. I longed to drown in my tears and fears when I remembered how far away from God I had strayed, yet I could not go any further. Like the prodigal child, in ignorance, enticed by the world, I leaned on my own understanding and left a palace of honor, great unseen riches, abundance overflow of wealth, and impenetrable protection. I left them all in search of an evil I did not yet know. When I expected death to find and reward me for my disobedience, I found eternal life instead and the grace of God helped me to believe in Christ for myself. The grace of God told me that there was no place I could have hidden that His eyes did not see.

I could write a billion more pages on the grace of God that kept me through it all. I could go on and on about the wars won and the battles lost, the joy seen and the regrets felt, but it would all end the same because He has been God through it all. I heard for a long time about the power of amazing grace, but it was not until I received it for myself that I believed it. So many wrongs committed, but God remained unchangeable in His love and grace. Now, I live to bask in that love and grace. This must have been the abundant life that Christ said He came to give. I was journeying through God's amazing grace all along. I wish I could say I found the grace of God, but I realize I never lost it. I was the one lost and it was His grace that found me. It was His grace that never gave up on me. To God be the glory for the faithfulness of His grace.

Wherever you are in your journey, whatever it is that you have done before this moment, I pray you allow me the grace to tell you that there is none beyond redemption. Nothing or no one can separate you from the love that God has for you. You may even be in a place where you do not feel that love and you are convinced that it does not exist, but I dare you to move closer to the voice that wants to pull you closer to Him away from the lies of the opposition and toward the eternal truth that is in Christ Jesus. God has been unchanging in His love and mercy since time began as we know it. Because His love is timeless, His grace knows no bounds. He did it for me, He will do it for you. This is a grace like no other, one that would go out of its way to encounter you and wait for you. I pray for you today as you continue your journey. I pray that the grace of our Lord Jesus Christ finds you and that you are given the courage to receive its fullness in Jesus name.

Thank you so dearly for walking this journey with me.

Printed in the United States
By Bookmasters